Praise for Kimberly A. Bowman

Wise woman Kim Bowman nails it in her new book, *The System We Never Built*, as she describes how our fragmented mental health system destroys families like hers and is dangerous for those it purports to help. Bowman shares her powerful memoir but goes well beyond by offering a deep analysis of what is wrong with our Revolving Door system and the blueprint to fix it.

Mindy Greiling served in the House of Representatives in Minnesota for 20 years. She has advocated for mental health since her son was diagnosed with schizo-affective disorder in 1999. Author of *Fix What You Can: Schizophrenia and a Lawmaker's Fight for Her Son*.

Kimberly is sharing with everyone her deeply personal and powerful message about the failures of our system to help her son. Sometimes, a personal story could move more mountains than legislation, but hopefully her story will bring solid change to an issue our society very much needs to deal with.

Despite all the resources, despite everyone she turned to, the system failed her son again and again. As a long-time advocate for mental health reforms, I'm hoping her message will resonate with policymakers, legislators, and those in the system that have power to make lasting change so that the story will have a better ending for other parents and those suffering from a mental illness.

We can and must do better. Kimberly's story can be a catalyst to make this happen.

Retired Ohio Supreme Court Justice Evelyn Lundberg Stratton, longtime advocate for mental health reforms, particularly in the criminal justice system.

The System We Never Build begins with a mother's deeply personal account of her son's journey through serious mental illness, but this is not just one family's story. Families across the country will recognize their experiences in these pages. Through more than a decade of navigating fragmented systems, Kimberly Bowman became an expert advocate out of necessity, learning firsthand what helped, what harmed, and what was missing when her son needed care. The result is both a compelling memoir and a practical guide for families seeking help for a loved one.

Bowman shares hard-earned lessons about navigating care, advocating effectively, and pushing for meaningful system change. For those of us who work in behavioral health, this book is also a powerful reminder of what our systems look and feel like from the perspective of the individuals and families who depend on them most.

Dr. Margie Balfour, MD and PhD in Neuroscience, co-author of the National Council for Mental Wellbeing's Roadmap to the Ideal Crisis System.

Kimberly Bowman has spent countless hours over several years advocating for her son to receive humane and effective treatment in his many encounters with the criminal justice and mental health systems. Dealing with corrections officers, prosecutors, defense attorneys, and mental health workers with the goal of getting her son released to appropriate mental health services has required persistence, determination, savvy, a very stubborn faith, and, of course, a mother's love.

In the "The System We Never Built," she generously shares the wisdom gleaned from these countless interactions. The result is a unique contribution to the literature of recovery and a *must read* for families, mental health advocates, treatment professionals, administrators, policy makers, and government leaders at every level who sincerely hope to be helpful in easing the struggles of persons afflicted with serious mental illness.

Dave Norman - Retired Public Defender Mental Health Specialist

THE SYSTEM WE NEVER BUILT

Severe Mental Illness, Criminalization, and the Fight to Create Real Care

KIMBERLY A. BOWMAN

KI
Productions

Paperback ISBN: 978-1-961605-72-5

Foreword by: Xavier Amador, Ph.D.

KI Productions & Publishing
Noblesville, IN

While this book has rattled around in my mind for over a decade, it couldn't be written until now. The content and lessons were still becoming my story. There is that question, when is the right time to begin sharing what one has learned? It felt too early in my journey, until now. There were things that still needed to unfold before I felt like sharing. This isn't to say that "I've arrived", because that is certainly not the case. Life lessons are continuing to unfold, and they will continue as long as I'm living and on this journey. But it just felt to me like it was now time to share this portion of my story.

That said, without the loving support of my husband, Larry, encouraging me to do it now, it may still be rattling around up in my head like a wishful thought waiting to be written. Behind me stands a strong and confident husband that really believes in me. I am so grateful for him and I wouldn't want to share this journey with anyone else. I'm grateful God allowed us to find each other at just the right time in our lives. Thank you for supporting me and this work that is so important to me.

Contents

Foreword

The System We Never Built is a courageous, heartbreaking, and urgently needed book. Kim tells the story of her son Jonathan with the honesty only a mother can bring, but this is not simply one family's story. It is the story of countless families who love someone with serious mental illness and discover, often in moments of crisis, that the "system" they were counting on was never truly built.

As a psychologist, and as someone whose own family has been touched by schizophrenia, I found this book both deeply personal and painfully familiar. Kim captures what so many families experience: the exhaustion of fighting for care, the terror of watching symptoms criminalized, the loneliness of being blamed or shut out, and the heartbreak of seeing a loved one fall through gaps that should not exist.

What makes this book so powerful is that it does more than expose failure. It insists on dignity, connection, accountability, and hope. Kim understands that people living with serious mental illness need more than emergency rooms, jail cells, and temporary fixes. They need treatment, housing, continuity, compassion, and relationships strong enough to survive fear and disconnection.

This is an essential book for families, clinicians, advocates, judges, law enforcement, policymakers, and anyone who wants to understand what serious mental illness does to a person, a family, and a community when care arrives too late—or not at all. Kim has written a book that bears witness, tells the truth, and calls us to build what should have existed all along.

Xavier Amador, Ph.D. Clinical Psychologist
Author of *I am Not Sick I Don't Need Help! - How to Help Someone with Mental Illness Accept Treatment* (Vida Press, 2026)

Part I

1

The Night Everything Changed

It was a Tuesday morning in early summer, the kind of day that starts with quiet predictability—coffee brewing, traffic humming outside, the sticky weight of humidity pressing against the windows. I had the local news murmuring in the background while I got ready for work, not really listening until I heard something that made my entire body still. A name. His name.

I turned toward the television, stunned. There, in the center of the screen, was my son's face. Only it didn't look like the boy I knew. It was a mugshot. Hollow. Expressionless. As if someone had drained the light out of him and left only the shell. My knees gave out beneath me, and I dropped onto the edge of the bed, gripping the comforter like a lifeline. I could hear my heartbeat in my ears, louder than the anchor's voice, louder than the world.

"Jonathan…," they said. "Apprehended after allegedly pointing a rifle from a downtown Lexington parking garage at pedestrians below."

My first thought wasn't about charges or consequences or reputation. It was just one desperate question: Is my son alive? I scanned the screen, listening for anything, hoping. Then I heard the word: Airsoft. It wasn't a real gun. He hadn't shot anyone. He was alive. Just like that, I exhaled the breath I didn't even know I'd been holding.

But it wasn't relief I felt—it was something else entirely. It was grief laced with fury, the kind of heartbreak that doesn't scream, but sinks its claws into your chest. What kind of life was this, I thought, where this counted as good news? Where my child's face on the news, linked to a terrifying incident, brought relief simply because he wasn't dead?

I grabbed my phone and called the station. When the producer picked up, I didn't hesitate. "You've got the wrong story," I said. There was a pause, and then she asked, "What do you mean?"

"I mean this isn't a story about crime," I told her. "This is a story about a young man with severe mental illness who didn't get the help he needed. The real story is how someone like Jonathan, despite our best efforts, could end up alone in a parking garage with an Airsoft rifle, untreated and invisible to the very systems designed to protect him."

But they didn't want that story. They wanted a clean narrative. Something sensational. Something to provoke a reaction. A crime. A public safety threat. Something that fit neatly into the evening news. There was no space in that broadcast for nuance, for illness, for broken systems or desperate mothers. So I called a friend at a competing network—someone who knew us, who had followed parts of our story over the years. That same afternoon, I was on their broadcast, telling the truth that the first station had ignored.

I explained that Jonathan had been diagnosed with a serious mental illness at a young age. That we had tried—truly tried—to get him help. That he had been turned away, discharged, misdiagnosed, and misunderstood. That we had knocked on every door, made every call, filled out every form. Yet he had still slipped through the cracks. Or maybe, more honestly, there weren't cracks at all—maybe the system just never had room for him in the first place.

We weren't a disengaged family. We weren't avoiding anything. Quite the opposite. As his mother, I fought hard to get him diagnosed correctly.... To get him medication prescribed....to get him help. It seemed that at every turn help is not what I found. No, not even collaboration. I was met with resistance, apathy, disinterest, at most every turn.

This book is about that failure. The quiet, persistent, devastating failure of the systems that are supposed to support individuals with serious mental illness. It is about what happens when care is conditional, when access is inconsistent, and when diagnosis becomes a sentence rather than a starting point. It's about my son. But it's not just about him.

How Did We Get Here?

Jonathan's story didn't begin with a rifle or a rooftop. It began with subtle signs, hard questions, and quiet fears.

I was a young mother—tired, uncertain, trying to keep up—and I remember pulling *The Strong-Willed Child* off my bookshelf in desperation when he was barely two years old. He wasn't just difficult; he was distressed. It was like his emotions were too big for his little body, and no amount of parenting tricks could bring calm to our days. By the time he was nine, even a trusted counselor at our church quietly suggested that we seek professional help. He gave us the name of a child psychologist, someone he trusted.

I am often asked what signs first concerned me. I could offer many examples, but if I distill them down as simply and honestly as I can, this is how I describe it: my son did not exhibit the emotions or reactions we typically expect to see. The positive and negative reinforcement parents rely on to shape behavior simply did not work for him.

I could take away his favorite activities or possessions, or try to motivate him with rewards that should have mattered to him —none of it made a difference. Those same approaches worked with his older brother. But not with him.

Quite simply, he did not respond to the hope of gain or the fear of loss in the way we expect from healthy, regulated behavior. And ultimately, that absence—no fear of loss and no hope of gain—is precisely what has contributed to years of his homelessness.

It only took a few sessions. The doctor looked at me with quiet seriousness and handed me a copy of *The Bipolar Child.* "I think you should read this," he said. That night, I read the entire book. Every page echoed my reality. It was as if the authors had written it with my son in mind. The behaviors, the mood swings, the volatility, the brilliance—it all matched. I felt validated and terrified all at once. Finally, a name for what we had been battling. Finally, a direction.

But naming the truth didn't make it easier. If anything, it made things harder. The psychiatrist we saw was compassionate but cautious. The medical director of the clinic didn't believe bipolar disorder could be diagnosed in children, which limited what she could formally document. There were concerns about the label following him for life, affecting his ability to get jobs, to serve in the military, to buy life insurance. One doctor even insinuated that some parents seek diagnoses to benefit financially from the system, as if our desperation was strategic. The implication stung more than I can say.

Meanwhile, Jonathan was being treated for conditions such as ADHD, major depressive disorder, and oppositional defiant disorder. But the correct diagnosis had not yet been identified. Unfortunately, mental health diagnosis often involves lengthy observation, evolving symptoms, and significant clinical interpretation. There is no objective blood test, for example, that can provide clear answers. As a result, his behaviors continued to intensify—because the underlying condition was not yet being treated.

Some reading this may recognize what I can only describe as a months-long nightmare. For those who are unfamiliar, diagnosing a mental health disorder often involves extended observation over time, gathering anecdotal information, and carefully measuring that information against detailed diagnostic criteria in the DSM-5. It means trying one medication. Then another. Trying a treatment approach. Then discontinuing it to attempt a different one. Creating medication "cocktails," each with its own side effects, and sometimes adding additional medications to counteract those side effects. More observation. More waiting. More trial and error.

I share this not as a medical professional, but from lived experience—because I want to set realistic expectations for anyone who may find themselves in the middle of this process. Even in the most stable families, this journey can feel overwhelming, disorienting, and at times, as though you are losing your own mind. You are not. I want to encourage you to stay the course. Don't give up. Managing through this process is incredibly difficult, but staying focused on the end goal—finding the right help for your loved one—matters.

In our family's case, this months-long process was especially exhausting and painful. With each new diagnosis and every change in medication, his behaviors worsened rather than improved. I measured how we were doing by how much his behaviors controlled our family's life. The more his behaviors dictated where we could go, when we could go, or how long we could stay, the more control he had—and the less we did.

The loneliness and isolation were real. Invitations slowly

stopped coming. When we did accept them, the stress of managing behaviors often made it easier to leave early—or not go at all. Many times, withdrawing and staying home felt like the only manageable option. Enduring the judgmental looks and comments from others became too much to bear.

I watched my son unravel before my eyes. It took nearly nine months before we pushed back, demanding they consider what we already knew to be true. When he was finally treated for bipolar disorder, we saw signs of progress within two weeks. His agitation softened. His thoughts slowed down. We had found a small foothold. It wasn't a cure, but it was a start.

We thought we were finally on a path to stability. But the cracks in the path would disappear only to return as manholes beneath our feet.

The System That Wasn't There

At fourteen, everything began to fall apart. Our family was navigating a painful divorce, and Jonathan spiraled. A friend helped me get him to a psychiatric facility, and I'll never forget the moment I had to leave him there. The strip search. The hollow echo of the door closing. The sterile feel of the room. I signed paperwork with shaking hands, praying this time would be different. Wondering as I drove away if I was doing the right thing leaving him there.

For a time, we tried everything. But after that first hospitalization, the instability never truly lifted. It felt as though I was no longer parenting—I was just managing chaos, and failing at it. I was desperately trying to find help, but I didn't know where to turn or even where to begin.

Then came the first overdose attempt. A cry for help. I was a mother doing everything she could to save her son, yet I felt completely lost—confused, overwhelmed, and deeply ashamed, as though I had failed him as a parent. Where was the instruction manual for this? Where was the safety net? Where was the hand reaching out to help?

One day, I came home to find my son's friend and her mother packing his belongings to move him out—into their home. I pleaded with her. "Please, you don't understand what you're doing. There are things you don't know." Nothing I said mattered. I stood there and watched as they drove away, leaving me broken, hurt, confused, and terrified.

A few short weeks later, I received the call I had always known would come—the call telling me to come pick him up. He was no longer welcome there. No one explained what had happened during those weeks. No one apologized for taking him before understanding the full situation. No one said, "We're so sorry. We didn't know what we thought we knew."

There was no support. No compassion.

He moved in with a neighborhood friend who introduced him to drugs, violence, and survivalism. Another toxic relationship, then after abusing and exploiting my son, that "friend" kicked him to the streets. He tried staying at a local homeless shelter. He called me the next morning. "I can't go back there," he said. "It's too dangerous." I believed him.

I scrambled. I worked my resources and coordinated services, secured a spot in a Crisis Stabilization Unit, organized a wraparound care team. For a year and a half, it worked. Barely. Then he moved in with another partner. When that ended, he was thrown out again. I made yet another call to a psychiatrist I knew. After spending more than two and half hours with my son, another diagnosis. This one is more severe than all the preceding diagnosis. With a phone call the Doctor secured him an admission at a local hospital with a mental health unit. But his behavior was so violent that they transferred him to a hospital better equipped to handle severe mental illness. It felt like a breaking point. Finally, a place that could give him real, sustained help. But within 72 hours, he was discharged. No acknowledgment of his schizophrenia diagnosis. No treatment plan. No stabilization. No safety net.

Because he was now eighteen, I couldn't even get details. HIPAA laws meant I was no longer legally entitled to information. I tried my best to provide the hospital with important information about my son and his history, but they wouldn't listen. They didn't want to hear or receive the information. All I knew was that my son was being released, again, into nothing. They claimed they were discharging him to a nearby homeless shelter, but I knew he wouldn't go there again, and I told them so. I pleaded with them to understand that they were really discharging him to the streets.

That was the moment his homelessness became permanent. That was the moment the system stepped away. This was the very moment and the decision that changed the entire trajectory of the next 12 years!

You Think It's Just You—But It's Not

For a long time, I believed our story was the exception. That we had somehow missed the one door that would have made a difference. But the more I've shared our experience, the more I've realized we were never alone. In fact, we were heartbreakingly common.

Research from mental health advocacy organizations suggests that millions of individuals with serious mental illness cycle through America's jails each year. According to the Treatment Advocacy Center, individuals with untreated mental illness are sixteen times more likely to be killed during a police encounter. Across the country, emergency rooms increasingly serve as holding spaces for psychiatric crises, with some patients waiting days for placement or treatment. Discharges happen without follow-up. Shelters turn people away. Families are left to pick up pieces they didn't break.

We don't treat mental illness. We punish it. We criminalize symptoms. We build courtrooms instead of clinics, and jails instead of beds. We fail people like Jonathan every day—and then we ask what's wrong with them.

There's a name for what's happening: the criminalization of mental illness.

It happens when we label a psychiatric crisis as a threat. When we call the police because there's no one else to call. When a young man ends up on the evening news not because he's dangerous, but because he's sick and untreated and desperate.

I will never forget one of my son's earliest interactions with law enforcement. In the early months of his unsheltered journey, he was living in a tent at a local campground. The campground was part of a much larger complex—so large, in fact, that it maintained its own police force.

Then came the call. Arrested.

I went to the campground to collect my son's belongings, searching for answers and trying to understand what had happened. I asked if I could speak with the arresting officer. When I tell you that, along this incredibly difficult journey we walk beside our loved ones, there are some truly good people we encounter—this officer is forever etched in my memory.

As he recounted the incident, he explained that he had approached my son's tent because the camping fee had not been paid. My son responded by pulling a knife and becoming wildly threatening toward him. When I say I am profoundly grateful for Crisis Intervention Trained (CIT) officers, I mean it with every fiber of my being. I owe my son's life to that officer.

He remained calm. He recognized the situation for what it was—a psychotic episode. A frightened young man experiencing a reality so real and so terrifying in his own mind that he believed he was under a life-threatening attack and needed to defend himself.

I still remember the chilling words the officer said to me:

"Ma'am, your son is very fortunate that it was me who responded to this call, and not one of my less experienced colleagues. The outcome could have been very different."

Instinctively, I knew exactly what he meant. An officer without CIT training. Someone less experienced. Less tolerant. Less self-controlled. Someone feeling threatened—perhaps even trigger-happy—and I might not still have my son. It is staggering for me to even contemplate.

I wish I could say this was the last such encounter. It was not. The number of times my son's life could have been taken is countless. I know about a few of them. I don't know about all of them—and this mother's heart doesn't want to know. I don't think I could bear it.

Jonathan's story is not unique. That is the tragedy. This is not a failure of parenting or persistence or love. This is a system failure. One that plays out every day, in every city, behind every locked hospital door and empty shelter bed.

We thought the help was out there. We believed if we just said the right words or found the right number, someone would catch him. What we didn't know was that every piece of the system was standing alone, waiting for someone else to take responsibility.

In that waiting, Jonathan fell.

2

A Maze With No Exit

They say the system is there to help.

But what they don't tell you is that the "system" is actually many systems—each standing alone, pointing to the next, waiting for someone else to take responsibility. When it comes to serious mental illness, those gaps aren't just frustrating. They're dangerous.

I remember sitting in a courtroom for eleven Tuesdays in a row, watching my son shuffle in and out in a jail-issued jumpsuit. Eleven weeks of holding my breath, hoping this would be the day someone saw him—really saw him. Eleven weeks of watching the same cycle unfold: no plan, no placement, no progress. On the eleventh week, the judge finally released him. Just like that. No treatment. No support. No one to catch him.

It was the end of June 2017.

Tim's Law, a promising new piece of legislation designed to allow court-ordered outpatient treatment for individuals with serious mental illness, was set to go into effect just days later—on July 1st. I held onto that date like a lifeline. But I would later find out that Tim's Law couldn't help us. Not yet. It had been passed without funding. The structure was there, but the resources weren't. So the law sat dormant while my son—my beautiful, brilliant, desperately ill son—was arrested again.

By our calculations, Jonathan was being arrested approximately every 11.6 days.

That wasn't a typo.

Every 11.6 days.

That number still haunts me.

I called the hospital. They told me to call the jail. The jail told me he needed a caseworker. The caseworker never called back. The outpatient clinic said he needed an assessment. The assessment couldn't happen without ID. He had lost his ID. He couldn't get a new one without a mailing address. He had no mailing address.

Round and round we went.

I kept thinking: this isn't a system. It's a maze. And it's a maze with no exit.

We had already been navigating this for over a decade. Twelve years of diagnoses and denials. Of discharge paperwork and prescriptions. Of showing up at emergency rooms, begging them to keep him, only to hear the same line: "He's not sick enough." Twelve years of trying to keep him alive while the system waited for him to "fail enough" to qualify for help.

That's the cruel irony—how badly someone must unravel before they are even considered for services that could have prevented the unraveling in the first place.

It's not just confusing. It's maddening. It is absolutely heartbreaking.

By the time Jonathan was finally offered AOT—Assisted Outpatient Treatment—it was through the Behavioral Health Docket, a specialized court modeled after drug courts. It took years of evidence: multiple incarcerations, hospitalizations, episodes of homelessness, failed interventions, and documented decline. Years. Only then was he considered "eligible" for the help he had needed all along.

The Behavioral Health Docket gave him what the broader system never did—structure, accountability, and compassionate oversight. It created a space where treatment could be enforced with support, not punishment. It brought together the wraparound services we had been begging for in one coordinated plan. It helped him stabilize—for a time.

But why did it take twelve years?

Why do we make people prove they're sick enough, broken enough, hopeless enough—before we help them?

What we call a "threshold" is actually a toll. A toll paid in lost time, lost potential, and too often, lost lives.

So many families are living this same nightmare. Getting bounced between mental health clinics, hospitals, probation officers, and social workers—each pointing in a different direction, none with the full picture. Every agency has a policy. Every provider has a protocol. But no one has a complete path. And certainly no one is carrying the weight the way a family does.

There is no warm handoff. There's just a cold goodbye.

There is no single entry point. There's a thousand dead ends.

It's not that no one cares. I've met good people inside the system. But good people can't do much when the system isn't connected. The reality is this: until we build systems that talk to each other, we are sentencing families like mine to years of chaos, trauma, and preventable harm.

My son didn't need another judge. He needed a bridge. And we shouldn't have to wait twelve years to find one.

decline. Years. Only then was he considered "eligible" for the help he had needed all along.

The Behavioral Health Desk gave him what the broader system never did—structure, accountability, and compassionate oversight. It created a space where treatment could be enforced with support, not punishment. It brought together the wrap-around services we had been begging for into one coordinated plan. It helped him stabilize, for a time.

But why did it take twelve years?

Why do we make people prove they're sick enough, broken enough, helpless enough—before we help them?

What we call a "threshold" is actually a toll. A toll paid in lost time, lost potential, and too often, lost lives.

So many families are living this same nightmare. Getting bounced between mental health clinics, the courts, probation officers, and social workers—each pointing in a different direction, none with the full picture. Every agency has a policy. Every provider has a protocol. But no one has a complete map. And certainly, no one is carrying the weight the way a family does.

There is no warm handoff. There's just a cold goodbye.

There's no single entry point. There's a thousand dead ends.

It's not that no one cares. I've met good people inside the system. But good people can only do so much when the system isn't connected. The reality is this: until we build systems that talk to each other, we are sentencing families like mine to years of chaos, trauma, and preventable harm.

My son didn't need another judge. He needed a bridge. And we shouldn't have to wait twelve years to find one.

3

This Isn't Just Our Story

After everything we went through—every unanswered call, every discharge, every time I was shut out by HIPAA or told "he's not sick enough"—I still thought maybe it was just us. That if I had done one more thing, said the right words, or found the right person, we could've saved Jonathan from what was coming. I carried that guilt for years, because when you're a parent, the world has a way of convincing you that if something goes wrong, it's because you failed to stop it.

I've learned something no one told me early on: it's not just us. It never was.

Jonathan's story—the missed diagnoses, the denied hospital beds, the revolving doors between jail and the street—is not the exception. It is tragically common. I've met so many other families, from so many walks of life, who carry the same exhausted stories. You start telling your experience, and someone across the table finishes your sentence. The settings may change, but the pattern does not.

This is not a personal failure. It's a systems failure—one that's happening all across the country.

Mental health advocacy organizations estimate that more than 2 million bookings involving individuals with serious mental illness occur in U.S. jails each year. That's not just a statistic—it's an indictment. It means that people with schizophrenia, bipolar disorder, and other severe conditions are far more likely to end up in jail than in a hospital. More likely to be criminalized than cared for. Jonathan lived that reality. He was discharged from hospitals too quickly, refused treatment too often, and then punished for the very symptoms he had begged for help managing.

How many times over 12 years, he reached the point of asking, seeking and willing to accept help, only to walk into an Emergency Department to receive the help, then to be turned away! Turned away from life saving medical help he so desperately needed.

The Treatment Advocacy Center reports that individuals with untreated serious mental illness are 16 times more likely to be killed by police during a law enforcement encounter. These aren't people who've committed violent crimes—many are experiencing psychiatric crises rather than criminal intent. They need medication and stabilization, not weapons drawn on them. Too often, we've forced first responders to become de facto mental health crisis teams without adequate training, resources, or long-term treatment alternatives. It's a recipe for tragedy.

If they survive the crisis and make it to the ER? That's no guarantee of care either. More than 1 in 10 ER visits today involve a behavioral health emergency, and the system isn't equipped to handle them. Instead of immediate treatment, patients are often "boarded"—held in emergency rooms for days due to a shortage of psychiatric beds. I've watched Jonathan sit for hours on a gurney, waiting for help that never came. We were told to be patient. Told there were no beds. Told he wasn't "urgent" enough.

I often reflect on a call I received from my son. He didn't sound like himself. He admitted that he had taken pills again. I rushed to his apartment and found him surrounded by pills scattered across the room. An empty liquor bottle nearby. My son was barely conscious.

I immediately called 911. Help arrived in the form of EMS and law enforcement. During the EMS assessment, my son asked me to tell his brother that he loved him. Even with the evidence of the attempt still visible—pills everywhere, the liquor bottle, the quiet goodbyes—EMS determined they were no longer needed. There was no immediate medical emergency.

With his vital signs stable, they quietly and unceremoniously left the scene.

That left law enforcement. The officer, aware of my background in mental health and my experience with the only dedicated inpatient psychiatric hospital in the region, said to me, "You know what will happen if we take him to the hospital." We both knew my son would not be admitted.

His advice was simple: stay with him through the night. Keep an eye on him.

I wish this were not a true story. I am left asking—what does "danger to self" really mean?

Even after a hospitalization, the risks don't disappear. A 2022 SAMHSA report found that less than 55% of adults hospitalized for serious mental illness received follow-up care within 30 days. Imagine undergoing a medical emergency, being stabilized, and then released with no follow-up appointment, no medication management, and no plan. It wouldn't happen to someone with a heart condition. But it happens to people with mental illness every day.

Jonathan was discharged multiple times with nothing more than a list of numbers to call. No coordination. No continuity. No connection. And when those numbers didn't work—or when we couldn't get past the waitlists or voicemail messages—he went without. That's not care. That's abandonment.

For many like him, homelessness soon follows. According to a 2023 policy brief by NAMI, about 30% of people experiencing chronic homelessness live with a serious mental illness. That's nearly one in three. These are not people who "refuse help." Often, they are people for whom no consistent help was ever available, people who have been rotated through programs that were never designed for their level of need, and who've been traumatized by care that came too late or too harshly.

We say they "fall through the cracks," but that language gives the system too much credit. These aren't cracks. They're chasms—deep gaps between disconnected agencies, inconsistent policies, and underfunded programs. Unless you have the energy, privilege, and persistence to build a bridge across those gaps, you lose your loved one to them. I've watched it happen. I've lived it.

Families like mine are told that we should be grateful—grateful for the brief hospitalizations, for the short-term therapy, for the hours we waited in emergency rooms. But survival shouldn't require this much fight. It shouldn't depend on whether your child gets a bed on the right day or whether a provider happens to pick up the phone. Yet it does.

Even now, with everything I've seen, I still believe we can do better. There are promising practices emerging—mobile crisis teams that respond with compassion instead of cuffs; housing-first models that stabilize people before expecting them to navigate recovery; peer support specialists who've lived through it themselves and know how to reach others. Research increasingly shows that these programs can reduce crises, improve stability, and save lives. But they're still the exception. We need them to become the rule.

We need to tell the truth: this is not about bad parenting. It's not about weak willpower or people who "don't want help." This is about a system that was never designed to hold the weight of real human need. A system that punishes symptoms instead of treating them. A system that expects mothers to act as case managers, nurses, advocates, and emotional shock absorbers—alone.

Jonathan didn't end up on the news because I failed him. He ended up there because every place I turned for help was either full, closed, not available, or silent. That's not just our story. It's America's story.

We can build something better. Not by accident—but by intention. That starts with naming what's broken, listening to the families living it, and refusing to accept a world where being mentally ill means being abandoned, arrested, or forgotten.

4

When Illness Becomes a Crime

After years of navigating broken systems—watching my son be discharged without follow-up, denied care because of paperwork, and punished for symptoms we couldn't treat—I started to feel something shift in me. I stopped asking, *What did we miss?* and started asking, *What kind of system lets this happen?*

That's when I heard a phrase I didn't know yet, but instantly recognized as true: The criminalization of mental illness.

Déjà vu. I thought we had already lived through a parking garage experience that ended in an arrest. We had. And here was another—this time exponentially worse.

My son, his appearance more dead than alive after living on the street—undernourished, unhealthy—approached a family in a parking garage. We don't know why. Maybe he was asking for a light for his cigarette. Maybe he was hungry and asking for help. Whatever the reason, the family warned him to stay back. He kept approaching. Warnings ignored.

The man pulled out a gun and aimed it at my son. According to the police report, a witness stated that the man was about thirty seconds away from firing if my son did not retreat.

When police arrived, they wrestled my son to the ground on the cold concrete. My son recalls telling the officers that he had undergone a medical procedure the day before and that they were tearing open his stitches. He was ignored. Restrained. Arrested—again.

The system did what the system does.

The criminalization of mental illness means this: when someone in a psychiatric crisis ends up in a jail cell instead of a hospital bed, when their symptoms are seen as defiance rather than distress, when families call for help and get handcuffs instead of healing—we are no longer treating illness. We are punishing it.

I didn't want to believe this was happening again. But it was. I received a call from a police officer I had built a relationship with. They usually called me first.

He said, "Kim, I'm here with your son again."

The officer explained why they had been called and asked if I had any ideas—anything they hadn't already tried. I wanted to scream. But at whom? I couldn't scream at the officer. He was trying to help my son, and he had run out of options.

We both knew what my son needed. He was sick, and he needed help. But in that town, getting him the care he needed felt nearly impossible. It was as if it would take an act of Congress to move decision-makers toward treatment instead of punishment.

Jonathan wasn't a criminal. He was sick. Yet time after time, the people who should have helped him treated him like a threat first. Whether he was pacing outside an emergency room, responding to voices only he could hear, or simply existing in public while visibly unwell, the response was rarely medical.

It was force.

It was suspicion.

It was control.

His earliest interaction with law enforcement happened when

he was just nine. He had wrapped a phone cord around his neck and ran barefoot into the woods. We called 911, terrified for his life. There were no mental health responders. No clinicians. Just police. No matter how kind they tried to be, they weren't equipped to understand what they were seeing.

That wasn't the last time we had to call for help. With each year that passed, the support we received got colder and more clinical—until eventually, it wasn't support at all. It was surveillance. Detainment. Courtrooms. Charges.

I still remember one of those Tuesdays, sitting in court and listening as the psychologist assigned to determine my son's competency to stand trial presented her testimony and findings.

She reported that during her evaluation, my son described being shot as a child—bleeding so severely that, in his mind, the wound eventually became a bee sting. As expected, the judge focused on her ultimate conclusion regarding competency. We were all prepared to hear not competent. Instead, she stated confidently, "Competent."

The courtroom fell silent—stunned, disbelieving. The judge engaged the doctor, asking the questions everyone else was thinking. Competent? You believe he is competent?

"Yes," she replied.

The judge then repeated her own findings back to her and asked again whether she truly believed this was a young man competent to stand trial for the charges against him.

I've shared before how grateful I am for certain people we encountered along this journey. This judge is one of them. As the presiding judge for the mental health court, he is a compassionate man who understands the complexity of cases involving individuals charged with crimes while also living with severe mental illness.

He flatly rejected the doctor's conclusion.

Common sense, though increasingly rare, does still exist.

This isn't just our story.

According to a 2022 report by the National Judicial Task Force, nearly 44% of people in jail have been diagnosed with a mental health condition. Many were arrested for low-level, nonviolent offenses like trespassing or loitering—often behaviors tied to untreated symptoms. Among incarcerated women, the rates are even higher. Research consistently shows that many individuals with serious mental illness enter the justice system through low-level offenses directly connected to untreated symptoms and instability. We are not locking up criminals. We are locking up people in crisis.

We've built systems that don't talk to each other—schools, hospitals, jails, courts—all standing alone, pointing fingers, waiting for someone else to act. There is no shared plan, no coordinated response. The more severe the illness, the more likely the person is to get bounced from one silo to the next until they land in a holding cell.

In many communities across the country, jails have effectively become some of the largest providers of mental health services. That alone should tell us something is deeply wrong. These are places designed for punishment, not healing. Yet we send our most vulnerable there—people who need consistent medication, stable housing, trauma-informed care—and then act surprised when they don't get better.

Jonathan didn't belong in court. He belonged in treatment. But time after time, when we tried to get him admitted to a hospital or clinic, we were told he wasn't "sick enough." Then, when his symptoms escalated into a public safety concern, suddenly he was "sick enough" to be charged, detained, and labeled a risk. It's a cruel paradox: not sick enough for services, but too sick for freedom.

And let's be honest—this criminalization doesn't happen evenly. People of color, particularly Black men, are disproportionately impacted. People living in poverty are more likely to be policed. People without housing, more likely to be arrested. When you add mental illness to any of those realities, the danger multiplies.

This isn't about individual bad actors. It's about a system that was never designed to hold people like Jonathan. We closed psychiatric hospitals without building community-based supports. We shifted funding away from long-term treatment and into temporary fixes. Now our jails are flooded with people who should have been helped years ago.

When the doors to psychiatric hospitals were suddenly closed, the intention was to provide community-based supports. But that system was not adequately planned, resourced, or built to meet the needs of those individuals requiring it. From then until now, gaps in services and providers are still desperately needed. Part of that strain is tied to an ongoing behavioral health workforce shortage, with too few trained professionals entering and remaining in the field.

We say they "fell through the cracks." But cracks imply an accident. This isn't an accident. It's an outcome.

Jonathan didn't stop being my son the day he was arrested. He didn't stop deserving compassion the day he became someone's "case." I didn't stop being his mother when the system stopped seeing him as a patient.

This is the criminalization of mental illness. It's real. It's systemic. And it is not acceptable.

We have to name it before we can change it.

5

When the Doors Close

Once someone like Jonathan is pulled into the justice system, it becomes even harder to bring them back into care. The criminal record doesn't just follow them—it blocks them. Housing applications. Treatment programs. Medicaid eligibility. And if they're also struggling with a serious mental illness, it's only a matter of time before the courtrooms turn into shelters, and the shelters turn into sidewalks. That's what happened to us. After the charges, after the discharges, after every door closed—Jonathan had nowhere left to go.

Homelessness wasn't the next chapter in his story. It was the collapse of the last one.

I don't think most people understand what homelessness really is—not until it touches someone they love. It's easy to drive past someone holding a sign and make assumptions. It's harder when the person on that corner is your son. When he used to sleep down the hall. When you remember the smell of his hair after a bath. The way he used to laugh during cartoons. The way he once looked for you in a crowded room and lit up when he found you.

Jonathan didn't become homeless because he made bad choices. He became homeless because anosognosia *(a condition where the brain can't recognize a mental health condition)* robbed him of the ability to have any insight into his mental health diagnosis. Because every service came with a condition he couldn't meet. Because mental illness stripped him of the ability to consistently follow rules he didn't understand. Because he got sick, and instead of being helped, he was managed, moved, and eventually forgotten.

We tried everything we were supposed to try. There was a period where he had housing—an apartment with wraparound support and a care coordinator. He was safe. Stabilized. Almost thriving.

But like so many people living with anosognosia, my son believed he was better and no longer needed medication. He wanted to know what life would be like without it. After all, he had taken medications—many of them—since he was a young boy. Why would he need medicine if he wasn't sick? And why would he need a team of professionals surrounding him? He believed their interest in him was driven not by care, but by their paid roles.

My son made the decision we had always feared he would one day make: he discontinued all treatment, including his medications.

As his mental health deteriorated and his illness made it increasingly difficult for him to trust providers, the services began to unravel. I remember his very first night in a homeless shelter. He called me the next morning and said, "I can't go back. It's worse than the street."

Based on what he described, I had to agree—at least in part. He was afraid that the few belongings he carried on his body would be stolen while he slept. He was surrounded by people exhibiting erratic or psychotic behavior, some intoxicated or drug-addled—or both. All night long, he worried that he might be physically assaulted by those around him.

That was the day everything shifted. From that moment on, he was unsheltered. Not by choice—but by default. Once someone reaches that point, every part of life becomes harder. You don't have a phone that stays charged. You don't have a fixed address. You miss appointments because of symptoms or sleep or fear. When you try to come back for help, you're told you missed your chance. The very things that made you homeless are then used as the reason you can't access support.

Homelessness isn't a crack people fall through. It's a chasm—a deep, structural failure of systems that stand alone: housing separated from health care, emergency response separated from treatment, law enforcement separated from compassion. When someone like Jonathan falls into that gap, climbing out without long-term, sustained help is nearly impossible.

According to the National Alliance to End Homelessness, over 30% of people experiencing chronic homelessness live with a serious mental illness. And that number is likely undercounted. These are people who were failed, not by their willpower, but by the systems that never made space for the way their minds work. They are not statistics. They are sons, daughters, sisters, parents. They are people with potential who have been pushed to the very margins of society.

Jonathan was assaulted while living on the streets. He was robbed. He was harassed. There were nights when he was arrested simply for being visibly symptomatic in public. He wasn't committing crimes. He was existing—loudly, erratically, confused—because he was sick. But instead of care, he got confinement. Instead of help, he got handcuffs.

I saw him once, standing on a street corner in the city where we both lived. He didn't see me. I just stared at him from a distance—he just looked so empty and forlorn. That's the day I realized I was mourning a son who was still alive. Because homelessness doesn't just take shelter. It takes presence. It takes memory. It erodes connection. It separates not just people from homes, but families from each other.

And perhaps the hardest part? He didn't want the help that was available to him. Not because he didn't want to be off the streets, but because he didn't trust the world anymore. He especially didn't trust me. After so many failed attempts at getting help, his illness told him I was part of the problem. That's what schizophrenia does when it's untreated. It warps reality. When your reality includes police lights and slammed doors, you stop believing safety exists anywhere.

I know I'm not alone. I've met mothers who keep socks in their cars in case they see their sons panhandling. Who store their child's medication in a trunk, hoping for a lucid moment. Who walk the neighborhoods near shelters at night, just to be close. These are not broken families. These are determined ones—doing everything they can while systems with power do nothing at all.

When people say "homelessness is a choice," I want to show them the trail of intake forms, the rejection letters, the waitlists. I want them to sit with me through the phone calls. To hear the ER nurse say, "There's nothing we can do." I want them to feel the moment when a mother's voice starts to crack—not from weakness, but from fatigue.

We did everything families are told to do. Still, it wasn't enough.

We don't just need more shelters. We need a new way forward. We need housing-first models that provide support, not conditions. We need embedded mental health care, long-term case management, peer support specialists, and outreach that meets people where they are. Research increasingly supports housing-first and integrated-care models as effective approaches for improving long-term stability among individuals experiencing chronic homelessness and serious mental illness. We need mental health care to be provided the same way any other healthcare is provided. We need the kind of care that believes people are worth investing in, even when they can't yet believe it themselves.

Because as it stands now, families like mine are left to search. To pray. To grieve while their loved ones are still breathing. To carry love into the places where the system no longer goes.

Jonathan didn't ask to be homeless. He asked to be helped. We couldn't give him what we never had access to ourselves. Until our systems are rebuilt—not just repaired, but reimagined—this story will repeat itself.

Not because of failure to love, but because of failure to act.

6

The Myths That Keep Us Stuck

They said he refused treatment. They said he was dangerous. They said he didn't want help. But what they didn't see was the fear in his eyes, the confusion on his face, the tremble in his hands as he stood in that parking garage with an airsoft rifle. What they didn't see was a young man, deep in the grip of psychosis, trying to survive a world that no longer made sense to him. He wasn't making threats—he was reacting to a threat he believed was real. He didn't know he was sick. He didn't think he needed help. And the system, in its cold and linear design, took him at face value and closed the door on him.

This is the danger of myth. It makes it easier to look away. It makes it easier to blame individuals instead of examining the broken systems that surround them. And it creates policy, funding decisions, and public perceptions that devastate real people—people like my son, people like our family.

Myth #1: "They Just Don't Want Help"

One of the most damaging myths is that people with serious mental illness (SMI) just "don't want help." The truth is, many simply can't recognize that they need it. My son wasn't refusing out of rebellion or laziness. His illness—specifically, the condition known as anosognosia—made it nearly impossible for him to perceive that he was sick. According to the Treatment Advocacy Center, about 50% of individuals with schizophrenia and 40% of those with bipolar disorder experience this neurological symptom. It's not a mindset—it's a malfunction in the part of the brain responsible for self-awareness. In those moments, Jonathan truly believed he was fine. He believed I was overreacting. He thought hospitals were traps. He didn't know what he didn't know. In those moments, he truly believed the world was out to get him. He believed everyone and everything was against him.

But instead of treating this as a medical reality, the system labeled it as defiance. He was called "noncompliant," "resistant," "unmotivated." These labels justified denying him services. They gave cover to the people and places that didn't want to deal with the complexity of his care. Each time, the refusal to intervene pushed him further into chaos.

I remember one of the times I tried to help him just before he became homeless. I was driving my son to the hospital to get help. He was floridly schizophrenic. A call from a psychiatrist had already paved the way for a bed and an admission—I just needed to get him there.

During the thirty-minute drive, I repeatedly worried that my son might try to jump out of the moving car or grab the steering wheel. I focused on keeping him calm, doing everything I could to make the ride safe.

While en route, I was on the phone with a social worker at the hospital we were heading toward. She was gathering as much background information as possible before our arrival. Even after I shared his full history and described the severity of his current psychosis, and while we discussed the very real possibility that he might refuse to enter the hospital once we arrived, she told me that because of his civil rights, "your son has a right to self-destruct, if that's what he wants to do."

Myth #2: "We Can't Intervene Because of Their Rights"

I want to be clear: I believe in civil rights. I believe in autonomy, dignity, and personal agency. But I also know what it looks like to watch someone slowly die with their "rights" intact. What we are doing in the name of liberty isn't freedom—it's abandonment. Over and over, I was told by clinicians, judges, and hospitals that their hands were tied. That my son had the right to refuse treatment, even as he descended into violent paranoia, lost housing, and was arrested again and again.

The problem wasn't always the law. More often, it was the fear of liability, the lack of clarity, the unwillingness to act without 100% certainty. Or it was the absence of a system prepared with services to meet the demand. And so, when bold leadership or clear guidance is missing, people like my son are left to fall—until they become dangerous enough to justify action. We need better standards. Clearer pathways. And the courage to say: sometimes, intervening is the most ethical thing we can do.

Myth #3: "Jail Is Safer Than the Streets"

I have heard professionals say it out loud: "At least he's not homeless. At least he's safe in jail." But that's a lie we tell ourselves because we've failed to build better options. Jails are not places of healing. For individuals with SMI, they are traumatic, disorienting, and often dangerous. They are placed in solitary confinement for "safety," denied access to necessary medications, and subjected to conditions that worsen their symptoms. According to the Bureau of Justice Statistics, people with mental illness are more likely to be physically assaulted while incarcerated, and they are more likely to die by suicide in custody than many other incarcerated populations.

My son has cycled in and out of these institutions. Each time, he came out more broken than before. He wasn't "safer." He was shattered.

Myth #4: "We Already Fund Mental Health Services"

People love to say, "Well, we've already put money into that." But I invite anyone who believes this to walk with me through a single week of trying to find care for my son. The money may exist on paper—but in practice, it is inaccessible, misdirected, and tangled in red tape. Oftentimes services in some communities are redundant, while in those same communities critical gaps remain. It's the gaps in services that are the most troubling.

Outpatient therapy for mild depression? Maybe. A psychiatrist in three months? Possibly. But try finding an inpatient bed for a young man in crisis, without private insurance, who lacks insight into his condition. Try getting a mobile crisis unit, if one even exists in your community, to come out at midnight on a holiday weekend. Try locating housing for someone who has a criminal record because the system criminalized his illness. The money is there, but it is trapped.

Research consistently shows that incarceration is significantly more expensive than providing appropriate community-based mental health treatment and supportive services. Incarceration fails to provide therapeutic value, and the outcomes are often worse. The money that is available rarely reaches the people who need it most.

Myth #5: "Families Should Handle It"

As a mother, this myth nearly broke me. People assume that if families cared enough, they would manage it all. That we're supposed to act as therapists, case managers, chauffeurs, guards, and emergency responders—all without burning out.

But let me be clear: families are doing everything they can. And still, we are losing people.

We are up late tracking them down. We are negotiating with hospitals. We are attending court hearings. We are draining savings. We are losing sleep. We are begging for beds. And we are blamed when the system fails.

What makes it worse? We are often willing to help, but not allowed to. HIPAA shuts us out. Providers shut us down. Attorneys are not trained and equipped in mental health matters. Judges don't listen. When things fall apart, the blame still lands on our shoulders. We are the last thread holding our loved ones together—and we're being asked to do it alone.

Myth #6: "He Chose This Life"

I've heard it more than once: "He made his choices." "He chose the streets." "He didn't want to follow the rules." But let's be honest—my son didn't choose to be ill. He didn't choose to have a brain disorder that interfered with his judgment, his stability, and his connection to the world. He didn't choose to have doors closed on him again and again. He didn't choose to live in a country where treatment is optional and jail is inevitable.

This is what happens when trauma, brain illness, poverty, and disconnection intersect. Stigma turns illness into moral failure.

And that false narrative becomes the reason we don't act. It becomes the excuse for inaction.

The Danger of Believing These Myths

These myths don't just live in casual conversations. They live in laws. They live in budgets. They shape how hospitals discharge patients, how judges rule on cases, how police respond to a crisis call. They affect how neighbors treat each other. They influence how news stories are told.

They create silence. They feed shame. They delay action. I've lived with the weight of them every day. I've seen how they changed the way people looked at my son. I've seen how they shaped assumptions about me as a mother. And I've watched how they influenced decisions that had devastating consequences for our family.

I am writing this to tell the truth. The myths are killing people. If we don't challenge them, if we don't name them, if we don't replace them with real stories and real data and real reform—then nothing will change.

But if we do?

We can build a system that sees people. That heals them. That catches them before they fall. That is why I keep telling our story.

7

The Cost of Misplaced Priorities

I asked about crisis housing. The case manager paused, then said, "We don't have any available in this community." I was stunned. This wasn't some wish-list service. This was a basic need—for people in crisis to have a bed, a door that locked, and someone to check in on them. But just like so many other times in my son's journey, the answer was: We can't afford that.

Later that month, Jonathan was arrested again. Booked into jail at $325 a night.

No one questioned whether we could afford that.

This is the contradiction we're living with. We say we care about mental health. We say prevention matters. We say we support families. But the truth lies in our budgets. When you look closely, the numbers don't lie. What we truly invest in—what we actually prioritize—is punishment, not prevention. Crisis, not care. Containment, not community.

Where the Money Is Going

Most people don't realize how lopsided the funding landscape is. At the local level, cities often allocate exponentially more to police and jails than to mental health care. In 2021, for example, Los Angeles allocated over $3.2 billion to policing, compared to just $521 million for mental health services—most of which went to contracted nonprofits with limited capacity. Many counties spend dramatically more on incarceration than on behavioral health.

At the state level, Medicaid carve-outs often push mental health management into the hands of third-party contractors, limiting transparency and creating administrative bottlenecks. In some states, entire regions lack access to crisis beds despite growing Medicaid expansion.

A lesser-known constraint, but just as detrimental for individuals receiving the help they need, is the IMD exclusion. The IMD exclusion is a Medicaid policy that prohibits federal funding for care provided to most patients in mental health facilities with more than 16 beds, significantly impacting access to inpatient behavioral health care.

Established in 1965, the IMD exclusion was intended to discourage large-scale institutionalization and promote community-based treatment models. However, over time, the policy has also contributed to significant barriers in accessing inpatient mental health care, particularly for adults between the ages of 21 and 64.

At the federal level, we do have the Substance Abuse and Mental Health Services Administration (SAMHSA), which provides grants to states and local agencies. But SAMHSA funding is often short-term, competitive, and narrowly focused—good for pilot programs, but not for building infrastructure. It's like giving someone gas money without buying them a car.

Imagine a pie chart of your city's spending. What would it show? In many places, it reveals our values with painful clarity: handcuffs are fully funded. Hope is not.

Cost Comparisons That Make You Pause

If we compare one example highlighted through Stepping Up Ohio in Delaware County, Ohio, the cost of cycling a single individual through public systems versus providing supportive housing and treatment reveals staggering differences. Public systems involvement for one individual over an eight-year period totaled more than $644,000, while supportive housing and coordinated services over that same period would have cost approximately $198,000. The difference—more than $445,000—reflects not only financial savings, but dramatically different human outcomes.

Let's break it down. A night in jail can cost between $100 to $500, depending on the facility. A night in a psychiatric hospital can cost significantly more. But supportive housing with wraparound services can cost a fraction of those crisis-driven interventions while often producing better long-term stability and outcomes.

An ER visit for a psychiatric emergency often costs thousands of dollars. A mobile crisis team response, on the other hand, can cost a fraction of that and may prevent hospitalization altogether.

Processing a single person through the court system—arrest, arraignment, detention—can cost thousands. But peer support programs and behavioral health courts, like the one Jonathan is now connected to, cost far less and have been shown in many communities to reduce recidivism.

Miami-Dade County in Florida offers a powerful example. Their jail diversion program for people with serious mental illness has reportedly saved millions of dollars annually by connecting people to treatment and support instead of incarceration. That's real money—and real impact.

Funding Failure, Not Prevention

Here's the hard truth: we are investing most in what fails people. We pour money into last-resort interventions—emergency rooms, jails, involuntary holds—and very little into early, sustained care. We react, rather than prevent. We treat crises but refuse to fund the stability that could avoid them.

My son was finally accepted into a program that was working. Jonathan was showing up. He had a case manager who understood him, a schedule he could stick to. For the first time in a long time, I felt a glimmer of stability. It took 12 long years of revolving and circulating between the streets, jails, and hospitals for him to finally get into a pretrial program, known by various names across communities, like Mental Health Courts or Behavioral Health Dockets. These are specialized courts for individuals with mental health disorders and justice involvement that qualify. But many communities still lack access to specialized behavioral health courts or diversion programs altogether.

This is what I mean when I say the system doesn't just fail people. Entire communities suffer the costs. How are we supposed to trust when there are so many barriers and obstacles to getting help?

Budgeting Without Lived Expertise

Who decides how these funds are spent? Often, it's people far removed from the daily reality of serious mental illness. It's finance directors. Elected officials. Department heads who have never sat in a psych ward lobby at 3 a.m., hoping your loved one will be admitted instead of arrested.

We need to center budgeting around lived experience. Families. Providers. Case managers. Individuals who've survived the system and want to make it better. These are the people who understand what actually works.

As one local advocate told me: "If you're not asking people who've lived it, you're budgeting blind."

The Hidden Costs We Don't Count

There are costs we can't capture in spreadsheets. Like the jobs lost by caregivers who have to miss work to go to court. Like the strain on marriages, the mental health of siblings, the children who grow up navigating trauma. The financial costs are staggering—but the emotional ones are often worse.

We lost more than money. We lost years. We lost birthdays. We lost trust. We lost time that will never be returned. And we lost pieces of ourselves along the way.

These are the hidden costs of a system that refuses to prioritize people. While they're harder to quantify, they are just as real—and far more lasting.

What Prioritizing People Could Look Like

It doesn't have to be this way. In Part II of this book, we'll explore what it looks like to truly invest in people—not just systems. But here's a glimpse of what's possible:

- Value-based funding that pays providers based on outcomes, not volume
- Community reinvestment of jail savings into treatment, housing, and crisis support
- Crisis stabilization centers funded at the state level, not just patchwork local efforts

• Medicaid innovation waivers that support wraparound services like job training, peer support, and transportation

These aren't pipe dreams. They're already happening—in places willing to shift priorities. What's missing is scale, will, and sustained investment.

The truth is, we're already paying. We just keep choosing the most expensive, least effective options. The longer we delay change, the higher the cost—for families, for communities, and for society.

In the next chapter, we'll look at the most devastating cost of all: what happens when we do nothing. The price of inaction is not just measured in dollars.

It's measured in lives.

8

The Danger of Doing Nothing

Winters were always the worst for me. Knowing my son was on the streets in subzero temperatures kept my mind in a constant state of hyper-concern. I knew Jonathan would not voluntarily go into a shelter. It seemed inevitable that whenever he did go into a shelter, he managed to break a rule—like going out to smoke when he wasn't supposed to—and get kicked out. I knew he chose to sleep over sidewalk grates to stay warm rather than go into a shelter. It was terrifying for me. It was especially terrible when the news reported another person found frozen to death. I always held my breath and hoped I wouldn't hear my son's name on the TV again.

I called the crisis line. I called the police. I even called the emergency room. Each call led to a dead end. One dispatcher told me, "He's not a threat to anyone." Another said, "We can't force him to go." One night, while doing what homeless people often do—walking for hours to stay warm and keep moving—Jonathan was struck by a distracted driver, suffering a neck fracture.

He was not only a danger to himself. That day, everyone was at risk. No one responded.

When One Person Falls, We All Feel It

When a person with untreated mental illness spirals into crisis, the impact extends far beyond that individual. A single psychotic episode can prompt multiple police responses. Violent arrests traumatize bystanders. Emergency rooms overflow. Families become isolated, overwhelmed, and afraid to ask for help.

These are not isolated personal problems. This is a national pattern of harm, one that touches nearly every layer of society. When systems fail, we all pay the price.

What the Research Says

The data paints a devastating picture. The Treatment Advocacy Center reports that a significant percentage of fatal law enforcement encounters involve individuals living with serious mental illness. According to the Substance Abuse and Mental Health Services Administration (SAMHSA), millions of people with serious mental illness are booked into jails each year in the United States.

Most people with mental illness are not violent. However, when psychosis is untreated and allowed to escalate, individuals become increasingly vulnerable—both to harm and to reacting in ways that may intensify encounters with the public or law enforcement.

The danger is not inherent in the diagnosis. It lies in the absence of care.

Inaction Leads to Instability

When nothing is done, instability grows. The system responds only when the crisis reaches a breaking point—through arrest, hospitalization, or tragedy. Requiring repeated failure as a condition for receiving help is inhumane.Homelessness increases. Emergency room visits and psychiatric readmissions spike. Incarceration rates rise. Costs skyrocket, while outcomes continue to decline.

Choosing inaction did not keep my son safe. It ensured that his fall would be harder, deeper, and more difficult to recover from, if I could just keep him alive through it.

The Trauma of Watching It Happen

Caregivers are forced into the role of helpless witnesses. Siblings become collateral damage. Friends drift away. I have known the pain of calling every agency I could find, begging for someone to help. I've waited in ER lobbies, begging for an admission, praying he wouldn't be discharged too soon. I've helplessly watched him unravel, knowing what was coming next and knowing there was nothing I could do to stop it.

This kind of repeated trauma leaves scars. Families are left with unresolved grief, symptoms of PTSD, and years of compounded emotional damage. I've spoken with other parents who stopped sleeping. Others who lost jobs, marriages, or homes trying to keep their child alive. The emotional toll is staggering—and rarely acknowledged.

What We Risk Losing Altogether

The cost of doing nothing is not just measured in financial terms. Every time the system fails to intervene, we risk losing people—

people who, with the right support, could thrive. We lose potential. We lose stability. We lose the chance to stop generational trauma before it begins.

Children watch their parents suffer without aid and grow up believing they will be abandoned too. Communities grow numb, distrustful, and disengaged. Public systems lose credibility, and families lose hope.

Every time someone says, "It's not my problem," the burden grows heavier for everyone else.

Tragedy as a Catalyst for Change

Reform often follows tragedy. High-profile deaths, lawsuits, or media investigations sometimes force public officials to act. After a shooting or suicide, new policies are drafted, new committees are formed. I've seen counties launch mental health courts only after a preventable death. I've seen law enforcement change protocol only after a child was lost.

These reforms matter. Yet they often come too late for the families already buried in grief. Systemic change should not require a public disaster. Listening and acting before tragedy strikes must become the new standard.

The Moral Imperative

At its core, this is not just a policy failure. It is a failure of values. A society that leaves its most vulnerable without protection has lost its moral compass. Families should not have to fight this hard to get basic care. No one should have to prove they are broken beyond repair to be taken seriously.

We cannot call ourselves compassionate while allowing systems to remain this broken.

We must ask: what kind of community are we building when

we allow people to disappear into psychosis, homelessness, or incarceration, simply because intervention is inconvenient?

This chapter marks the end of Part I—the truth-telling, the unveiling, the personal and systemic breakdown of a mental health crisis that has gone unanswered for far too long.

The danger of doing nothing is that it guarantees more of the same: more suffering, more loss, more silence.

Yet the moment we choose to act—something better becomes possible.

Part II

9

Building the System from the Ground Up

I used to think we just needed to fix the gaps. A little more funding here, a new therapist there, maybe some better coordination. But after twelve years of watching my son fall through every piece of a disconnected system, I've stopped believing in patches.

The system isn't broken. It was never built for people like Jonathan in the first place.

He was expected to ask for help before he knew he needed it. He was required to fail over and over again to prove his need for support. He was criminalized for behaviors rooted in untreated illness. What we call a "mental health system" is really a collection of loosely connected agencies, programs, and laws—none of which are truly built to respond to serious mental illness with consistency, humanity, or urgency.

It's time to stop rearranging pieces and start designing the structure to work. We must build something new.

From Patchwork to Purpose

Right now, mental health response looks different in every county, every city, every courtroom. Some families get access to coordinated care. Others receive nothing but voicemail boxes and rejection letters. Most of us are left chasing resources, researching services, pleading with strangers to see our children as human, not dangerous.

A system that depends on geography, luck, or whether a judge is having a good day is not a system. It's a gamble.

What we need instead is a national framework that guides coordinated, compassionate care across all levels—emergency response, hospitalization, outpatient treatment, housing, and long-term support. This isn't just about expanding services. It's about anchoring them in values we can stand behind.

What Should Guide Us

If we are going to rebuild, we must begin by asking: What should this system stand for?

We must design a mental health infrastructure that is:

- Proactive, not reactive
- Collaborative, not siloed
- Grounded in dignity, not denial
- Accessible, regardless of insurance or zip code
- Centered on care and healing, not containment

This means creating a system that acts before someone is forced to hit rock bottom—not after.

A Map Already Exists

We are not starting from scratch. Tools like the Sequential Intercept Model already offer a roadmap. This model identifies multiple key intercept points where individuals with mental illness can be diverted from the justice system and connected to care:

1. Community services (prevent crisis before it happens)
2. Law enforcement/crisis response
3. Initial detention and court hearings
4. Jails and specialty courts
5. Reentry support
6. Community corrections and long-term services

Programs like Assisted Outpatient Treatment (AOT) and Behavioral Health Dockets (like the one that finally helped Jonathan) are examples of what's possible when intervention is structured and sustained.

The problem is not a lack of models. The problem is the lack of will to adopt, fund, and scale them.

Rebuilding Means Integrating

To rebuild the system, we must bring together what currently exists in fragments:

- Hospitals must be connected to housing providers
- Courts must be linked with clinicians
- Families must be considered part of the care team, not obstacles
- Law enforcement must coordinate with mobile crisis units and peer support teams

No one should leave a hospital without a discharge plan that includes treatment, housing, and a follow-up contact. No one should be arrested without a mental health screening. No family should be denied participation in care planning due to overly restrictive or inconsistent interpretations of HIPAA.

This is not just a policy shift. It is a cultural one. We need a new paradigm.

A Missed Opportunity

I remember the particular hospital discharge that had a deeply significant impact on my son's future and the trajectory of his illness. This was the discharge that changed everything. After witnessing my son having his first major psychotic break, complete with paranoia and voices, I took him to see a personal friend and colleague who happened to be a very well-respected psychiatrist in our area.

After spending hours with Jonathan, he took me aside and told me my son was experiencing florid psychosis, which is a psychotic disorder characterized by severe hallucinations, intense delusions, and disorganized thinking. He believed the correct diagnosis was now schizophrenia.

A second psychiatrist examined my son and concluded the same diagnosis. Within 24 hours of those two doctors, he was transported involuntarily to a psychiatric hospital capable of treating him safely. Following the mandatory psychiatric hold, instead of providing a path forward to treatment, that hospital chose to discharge my son to the streets instead.

That is when the nightmarish journey of homelessness really became permanent for the next 12 years.

I just remember how hard I fought for them to keep him. I made phone calls to as many people with influence as I could find. But my efforts had no impact on the outcome.

It wasn't long after that before he ended up in jail for trespassing—lost, confused, and afraid.

Had there been a process that connected the hospital to a local mental health court or crisis stabilization program, the outcome would have been different. Jonathan would not have ended up behind bars. I would not have had to drive to court and watch him appear in shackles for simply being sick.

Rebuilding means preventing moments like that—not responding after the damage is done.

This Is Not Too Big to Change

Some will say the problem is too big. Too expensive. Too complex. But this country has rebuilt before. We have overhauled systems when we've had the courage to name their failure and imagine something better.

We did it with child welfare. We did it with veterans' care. We are capable of doing it again for mental health.

The truth is, we cannot afford not to change. The current system costs us billions in incarceration, emergency care, and lost productivity—not to mention the incalculable human toll.

THE NEXT CHAPTERS will outline specific solutions—programs that work, laws that need changing, and policies that honor the lives we're trying to save. Change begins here—with a decision to stop tweaking and start building.

We are not helpless. We are not alone. We are not out of options.

The path forward begins with the belief that something better is possible—and the courage to demand it.

10

What Real Support Looks Like

After years of watching my son cycle through jail cells, emergency rooms, and hospital discharges that led to nowhere, I used to wonder—does anyone actually know what effective help looks like?

The answer is yes. Real support systems do exist. Some counties have them. Some cities are building them. Families like mine have fought to create them. Unfortunately, access depends entirely on geography, political will, and whether or not someone in power believes your loved one is worth saving.

We know what works. We just don't fund or scale it.

From Talk to Treatment: What Actually Helps

We've seen decades of lip service: "mental health matters," "stigma kills," "check on your strong friends." Words without action don't save lives.

Effective support for people with serious mental illness isn't vague. It's not random acts of kindness. It's structured, evidence-based, long-term care. Here's what that looks like:

Assisted Outpatient Treatment (AOT)

AOT PROVIDES court-ordered outpatient treatment for individuals with serious mental illness who meet specific criteria—typically a history of repeated hospitalizations or incarcerations. It balances personal liberty with the reality of impaired decision-making.

It's not a magic fix, but when implemented well, it reduces hospitalization, arrest, and homelessness. Studies cited by the Treatment Advocacy Center have shown AOT programs reduce hospitalization rates by significant margins in many jurisdictions, with some studies reporting reductions greater than 50%.

Jonathan eventually became eligible for AOT through the Behavioral Health Docket in the county where he was homeless. For the first time, he had structure, follow-up, medication monitoring, and people who actually checked in to see if he was okay. It shouldn't have taken twelve years to get there.

Assertive Community Treatment (ACT)

ACT IS a team-based model that brings care to the person instead of waiting for the person to come to care. The teams usually include psychiatrists, social workers, nurses, and peer specialists, available 24/7. ACT works especially well for individuals who struggle to engage with traditional outpatient models. Failing isn't punished. Striving for recovery means relapses are expected. People are supported through the relapses.

According to SAMHSA, ACT programs can reduce psychiatric hospitalization by as much as 40–50%. Yet ACT is still unavailable in many rural counties, and implementation varies widely by state.

Crisis Stabilization Units & Mobile Crisis Teams

INSTEAD OF DEFAULTING to police or jail, crisis stabilization units (CSUs) provide short-term, hospital-like care for people in crisis—without handcuffs or criminal charges.

Mobile Crisis Teams, often staffed with clinicians and peers, can de-escalate situations on-site and divert individuals from emergency rooms. Cities that have implemented these teams—such as Eugene, Oregon's CAHOOTS model—have seen cost savings and better outcomes. According to the White Bird Clinic, CAHOOTS saves the city of Eugene an estimated $8.5 million annually in public safety spending.

Jonathan didn't have access to mobile crisis response when he needed it most. Instead, he was met by officers trained to detain, not de-escalate. That distinction changed everything.

Supportive Housing Programs

PERMANENT SUPPORTIVE HOUSING combines housing with on-site mental health services. It reduces homelessness, improves stability, and keeps people out of jails and hospitals. According to multiple supportive housing studies, these models can significantly reduce public-system costs while improving long-term housing stability and health outcomes.

I have seen what happens when someone like Jonathan gets even a few months of stable housing and support. His symptoms lessen. His fear decreases. His compliance improves. The challenge is sustaining it.

Real Support Wraps Around the Person

ONE-TIME PROGRAMS DON'T WORK. People with serious mental illness often need wraparound services that follow them through every stage: from discharge to housing, from therapy to medication support. This requires case managers who are trained and paid well enough to stay. It requires systems that don't drop people once the funding cycle ends.

Support must be relational, not transactional. It must be built for continuity—not convenience.

Accountability Without Punishment

SYSTEMS LIKE BEHAVIORAL HEALTH COURTS—LIKE the one Jonathan eventually accessed—can work when they provide structure without criminalization. The goal is not to punish people into compliance, but to help them develop the insight, stability, and supports needed to stay well.

This model works. According to research by the Council of State Governments Justice Center, mental health courts have been associated with reductions in recidivism and improved treatment engagement in many communities.

I know specialized courts are not the right solution for everyone. But for my son, it is working.

For the first time in his life, I am able to have a truly meaningful relationship with him. He is housed. Warm. Fed. Safe. He has wraparound support from an entire team—professionals who are there to support him, not punish him.

My son is calm, clear, and lucid. He is rational, teachable, and self-controlled. He is conversational, thoughtful, and articulate. I have not seen him doing this well since he was a teenager, when life was simpler.

We have hope. He now has things he values—and he does not want to risk losing them.

That said, no program is perfect. If I could suggest improvements to the Behavioral Health Docket, I would encourage making the time spent in the program more intentional and more rehabilitative. Until a person gains meaningful insight into their illness and is willing to voluntarily engage in the treatment that helps them remain stable, the hope that sustains families remains fragile.

Without continued medication, treatment, and support, there is little reason to believe stabilization will endure once someone graduates from the program. The time spent in these courts must be used strategically—maximizing services, strengthening insight, and building long-term supports that set individuals up for sustained success.

If someone continues to believe they are not ill, then once the mandatory phase of treatment ends, it is reasonable to expect a return to illness.

Things are not perfect. We still have concerns. But from where we stand today, the future looks brighter than it has in a very long time.

What Real Support Requires

Here's what all of these models have in common:

- Consistency
- Coordination
- Community investment
- Courage to do things differently

This work cannot depend on overworked ER doctors or parents calling 17 numbers in a panic. It requires funding, training, and infrastructure designed to meet the needs of people with severe mental illness—not just those with insurance or insight.

We Know What Works. The Question Is: Will We Choose It?

These models are not theoretical. They exist. They've been tested. They've changed lives. The question now is whether we will stop ignoring them, underfunding them, or limiting them to a few pilot programs.

What real support looks like is not a mystery. It's a decision.

11

Changing the Laws That Hurt More Than Help

After my son was arrested, hospitalized, and released over and over again, I kept hearing the same explanation: "Our hands are tied."

I was told he had rights. He had the right to refuse medication. The right to leave the hospital. The right to decline services. I was also told I could not be involved in his care unless he signed a release form—which, in the middle of a psychotic episode, he was never going to do.

These weren't just frustrating roadblocks. They were life-threatening ones.

Many of the laws we rely on to protect civil liberties were written before we fully understood the neurobiology of serious mental illness. They weren't designed for psychosis. They weren't designed for people who lack insight into their condition. They were written with the best of intentions—but often lead to devastating outcomes.

We need to reexamine the laws that make it nearly impossible to intervene until it's too late.

The "Right to Refuse" Doesn't Always Mean the Right to Recover

There is a difference between choosing not to take medication and being neurologically unable to recognize that you need it. Yet the law rarely makes this distinction.

Anosognosia—a medical term meaning "lack of insight"—is a symptom of many serious mental illnesses, including schizophrenia and bipolar disorder. It is not denial. It is not defiance. It is a brain-based impairment that prevents someone from understanding they are ill.

When someone is actively psychotic, their ability to make informed medical decisions may be impaired. Yet our current legal structure often treats every refusal as a conscious choice rather than a medical symptom.

Refusing care in the middle of psychosis is not informed consent. It's a crisis waiting to happen.

HIPAA: Help or Hurdle?

I have no issue with protecting privacy. However, HIPAA laws are very often misunderstood or misapplied, especially during mental health crises.

When my son was hospitalized, I was told they could not speak with me. When he was released, I was not notified. When he missed appointments, I was left out of the loop. This lack of information put him—and others—at greater risk.

HIPAA does allow providers to share information with family members if the patient is incapacitated or if disclosure is in the patient's best interest. Sadly, many institutions interpret HIPAA in the most restrictive way possible, either out of confusion or fear of liability.

Families are not the enemy. We are often the only consistent support system in a person's life. Shutting us out helps no one.

The "Danger to Self or Others" Standard Is Failing Everyone

Most states require that a person pose an immediate danger to themselves or others before involuntary treatment can be initiated. This legal threshold was designed to protect against abuse and overreach, but in practice, it forces families and providers to wait until a crisis explodes.

By the time someone meets the legal standard for danger, the damage is already done.

Waiting until someone becomes violent, suicidal, or dangerously psychotic is not compassion—it's negligence dressed up as liberty.

We need legal mechanisms that allow for earlier, medically informed intervention when someone is clearly deteriorating. Court-monitored outpatient treatment, expanded civil commitment criteria, and updated psychiatric advance directives are all options worth exploring.

When Good Laws Go Unfunded: The Case of Tim's Law

It was 2017. I sat in court for the eleventh week in a row. Jonathan was not improving. The judge had little power to act. I kept waiting for something to change.

On July 1st, Kentucky's Tim's Law was set to go into effect. Named after a young man with untreated schizophrenia who died after years of suffering, the law would allow for court-ordered outpatient treatment for people like my son. It was a glimmer of hope. There was one problem: the law had passed—but it wasn't funded.

It would be years before Tim's Law could be implemented with consistency. In the meantime, Jonathan was arrested again. And again. On average, every 11.6 days. According to local reporting and court records from that period, the cycling between arrest and release had become relentless.

Passing laws is not enough. If there is no infrastructure to enforce them, families are left with empty promises.

What Needs to Change

Reform must include not just what the law allows, but how the law is applied in real life.

• Clarify HIPAA for families and providers during psychiatric emergencies.

• Revise civil commitment laws to reflect medical realities like anosognosia.

• Support psychiatric advance directives so individuals can express their treatment wishes before a crisis.

• Fund and expand outpatient treatment models like AOT and Behavioral Health Dockets.

• Train judges, public defenders, and law enforcement to recognize mental illness and make diversion the default, not the exception.

Families Shouldn't Have to Become Lawyers to Save Their Loved Ones

I've sat through court hearings I didn't understand. I've read legislation I didn't know how to interpret. I've written letters, filed petitions, made calls, and begged strangers to help me keep my son alive.

The people most affected by these laws—those of us on the front lines—are often the least equipped to navigate them.

This has to change.

Laws should not be written in ways that protect systems over people. They should not favor bureaucratic liability over clinical reality. They should not ask caregivers to remain silent while watching someone deteriorate in plain sight.

Every law school should require dedicated instruction on mental illness. Given how prevalent mental health conditions are, it is more likely than not that attorneys will represent a client living with a psychiatric diagnosis at some point in their careers.

Over the years, I have worked with many attorneys. When I encounter one who truly understands mental illness, the difference is profound. That attorney is positioned to pursue what is genuinely best for my son—not simply what is most expedient in order to move a case along and check another name off a client list.

The same holds true for prosecutors. When prosecutors understand mental illness, they are better equipped to recognize when treatment—not incarceration—is the appropriate response. That understanding can mean the difference between steering someone toward a Behavioral Health Docket and sending them to jail.

Policy That Protects Life Over Liability

There is a way forward. Several states are exploring reforms that balance civil liberties with public safety:

- California's CARE Court program, launched in 2023, offers court-ordered plans for treatment, housing, and services, while giving families a formal role in initiating support.
- New York's Kendra's Law has expanded access to AOT, with studies showing reduced hospitalizations and arrests.

- Federal grants through SAMHSA's Mental Health Block Grant are helping states develop crisis response systems and expand community-based care.

These are steps in the right direction—but progress remains uneven, and too many families are still stuck in legal quicksand.

Laws reflect values. Right now, our laws say that people like Jonathan have the right to suffer in silence. The right to spiral alone. The right to refuse help they do not understand they need.

That is not justice. That is abandonment disguised as protection.

If we want a system that truly cares for its most vulnerable, we must write laws that make care possible.

12

Centering Families and Lived Expertise

Despite spending every waking moment trying to keep my son safe, I was often treated like a bystander. I've had conversations with caseworkers, judges, and doctors where I felt insignificant, irrelevant, and ignored. Decisions were made without me. Discharges happened without my knowledge. Plans were discussed in rooms I wasn't invited into—rooms full of people who barely knew his name, while I sat outside holding years of documentation, diagnoses, and history.

The message was clear: Your lived experience matters less than our professional credentials.

I've come to believe the opposite. If we want systems that actually work, families and people with lived experience must not only be invited—they must be centered.

The Expertise You Can't Learn in School

No one understands the reality of mental illness like the people living with it—and the families walking beside them. We are not simply emotionally invested. We have information that matters.

We've tracked symptoms for years. We know how a certain medication affects appetite or mood. We've seen how our loved ones respond when a stranger enters the room. We've intervened in emergencies. We've de-escalated situations before the police arrived. We've advocated, researched, begged, and persisted when the system shut its doors.

That is expertise.

Lived experience is not anecdotal. It is data—hard-earned, deeply contextual, and critically important to decision-making.

A System That Pushes Us Out

Too often, the system treats families as obstacles.

- HIPAA is interpreted to exclude us, even when we are the primary caregivers.
- Discharge plans are made without input, even when the patient is returning to our home.
- Schools, courts, and providers withhold information, sometimes not only to protect the individual, but also to protect the institution.

In my journey, I have been told I was overreacting, codependent, controlling, and uninformed. I have been dismissed by clinicians who spent thirty minutes, sometimes less, with my son after I had spent years documenting his decline. I have been asked to transport him to appointments, then excluded from the conversation once we arrived.

Families should not have to fight to be taken seriously.

The Value of Peer Support and Lived Perspective

One of the most powerful interventions I've seen isn't medical at all—it's relational.

Peer support specialists—individuals with lived experience of mental illness or caregiving—offer connection that professionals often cannot. They help rebuild trust, reduce shame, and model recovery. Programs that embed peer support into mental health systems report higher engagement, reduced hospital readmissions, and better long-term outcomes.

According to SAMHSA, peer support services are associated with increased self-efficacy and reduced use of inpatient services. Yet, these roles are often underpaid, undervalued, or tacked on as an afterthought.

If we want compassionate, effective care, we must elevate the voices of those who have walked the road.

Families as Co-Designers, Not Afterthoughts

True system reform must include families as:

- Co-creators of care plans
- Members of advisory boards
- Participants in policy review
- Leaders in advocacy and training
- Partners in crisis response

Some communities have begun to do this. In New York, Family Resource Centers offer education, navigation, and peer support to help families engage meaningfully. In California's CARE Court model, families can petition for structured care on behalf of a loved one—recognizing that sometimes, we see the crisis coming before anyone else does.

Including families does not mean ignoring the rights of individuals. It means designing systems that are relational, not transactional. Systems that build bridges, not walls.

A Team That Finally Listened

Along this journey, there have been a few moments when I truly felt heard—when my perspective was valued and I was included in decisions about my son's care.

Perhaps the most significant was when I found myself in conversation with both my son's public defender and the prosecutor on the other side of the case, at the same time. It is no small thing to support a loved one when both sides of the courtroom can be brought to the same place—aligned not against each other, but alongside the person living with mental illness.

That shared alignment must center on what is genuinely best for the individual, not merely on the rigid application of the law. When legal professionals move beyond simply checking procedural boxes and instead ask how the law can serve as a tool to support treatment, stability, and recovery, meaningful change becomes possible. Without that shift, the same destructive cycles repeat themselves.

It is remarkable what can happen when someone is seen first as a person living with illness who needs help—rather than as a criminal to be processed.

That moment changed everything.

I didn't expect them to do exactly what I said. I simply wanted to be heard. For once, I felt like a partner—not a problem. That one moment of inclusion led to a more thoughtful care plan, a smoother transition, and a better outcome for my son.

What Inclusion Looks Like in Practice

To truly center lived experience, we need:

- Training for professionals on how to collaborate with families and peers

• Family engagement policies that clarify HIPAA and support transparent communication

• Peer support programs embedded across the system—not just in recovery centers, but in jails, hospitals, and crisis response teams

• Funding for family navigators who can help others through the maze

This is not charity. This is infrastructure. Families and peers should be compensated for their time, trained for their roles, and treated as central—not supplemental—to the mental health workforce.

I am not just a mother who worried. I am a woman who fought for years, through systems that asked me to be both silent and responsible.

I kept my son alive long enough for the system to finally see him. I showed up when it was inconvenient. I asked questions no one wanted to answer. I held hope when the system had none to offer.

That is expertise.

If we want mental health care that heals, we must trust the people who have been doing the work all along. Families. Peers. Survivors. Caregivers. We are not outside the system. We are the system. It is time we were treated that way.

13

Innovation on the Ground

Every time I sat in a courtroom or emergency room hallway, I wondered: Is there anywhere doing this differently?

After years of watching my son fall through the cracks, I began to look for communities that weren't just waiting for tragedy—they were actively preventing it. And I found them.

Scattered across the country are places where leaders, clinicians, families, and advocates have decided to build systems of care that are smart, humane, and effective. They didn't wait for perfect legislation or unlimited funding. They started where they were—with people, partnerships, and the will to do better.

These stories remind us: we don't have to accept the system as it is. Change is not only possible—it's already in motion.

Miami-Dade County, Florida: Diverting from Jail to Care

Judge Steven Leifman saw the pattern clearly: people with mental illness were being jailed over and over for low-level offenses—

trespassing, loitering, disorderly conduct. They weren't criminals. They were sick.

Instead of accepting the status quo, he helped launch one of the most effective jail diversion programs in the country.

Miami-Dade's Criminal Mental Health Project diverts eligible individuals with serious mental illness out of jail and into community-based treatment. The results speak volumes:

• Over 5,400 people diverted since its launch

• Reduced recidivism by significant margins in participating populations

• Saved taxpayers millions of dollars annually through diversion and treatment-focused approaches (Source: Eleventh Judicial Circuit of Florida)

Even more inspiring, the county reinvested jail closure savings into building a Mental Health Diversion Facility—an alternative to incarceration where people receive treatment, housing, and support under one roof.

It's working. It started with one judge asking a better question: What if we treated mental illness like an illness?

Eugene, Oregon: Mobile Crisis Done Right

For over three decades, the city of Eugene has run CAHOOTS (Crisis Assistance Helping Out On The Streets), a mobile crisis team staffed by a medic and a mental health crisis worker—not police.

When someone calls 911 for a mental health concern, CAHOOTS responds if no weapons or violence are involved. The team de-escalates, offers support, and connects individuals to services. There are no handcuffs. No jail cells. Just help.

The results:

• A substantial number of crisis-related calls diverted away from traditional police response

• Estimated $8.5 million in annual public safety savings (Source: White Bird Clinic)

CAHOOTS shows what happens when we stop treating mental illness as a law enforcement problem and start treating it as a public health issue.

San Antonio, Texas: The Bexar County Model

San Antonio didn't just change one part of the system—it connected all of them. The Bexar County Mental Health Consortium brought together law enforcement, hospitals, judges, and behavioral health providers to redesign how their community responds to mental illness.

Their innovations include:

• A 24-hour Crisis Care Center

• Jail diversion programs embedded in booking facilities

• Training for law enforcement officers in Crisis Intervention

• A public campaign to reduce stigma and promote early intervention

In the first several years, Bexar County reported substantial savings in jail costs while also reducing recidivism and increasing access to treatment.

What makes their model powerful isn't just the services—it's the coordination. Everyone is talking to each other. Everyone is rowing in the same direction.

New York's Kendra's Law: AOT with Accountability

Passed in 1999, Kendra's Law allows courts to order Assisted Outpatient Treatment (AOT) for individuals with serious mental illness and a history of hospitalizations or violence. While controversial to some, studies consistently show reductions in hospitalization, incarceration, and homelessness among participants receiving structured outpatient support.

New York's model is built around consistent care, medication management, and court-monitored compliance—with support teams that include case managers and clinicians. This isn't about punishment. It's about protection—of the individual, their family, and the community.

Other Bright Spots Across the Country

- Colorado: Investing in co-responder teams, where police and mental health professionals respond together
- North Carolina: Expanding peer respite centers, offering short-term voluntary crisis care
- California: Launching CARE Court, a civil alternative to conservatorship that includes family input
- Georgia: Growing clubhouse models like Skyland Trail that offer long-term community and skill-building for people with SMI

A National Effort to Rethink the System: The Stepping Up Initiative

In recent years, some communities have begun to recognize that the cycle of arrest, incarceration, and release for people with serious mental illness is not only ineffective but deeply harmful. One initiative that has helped shift this conversation is the Stepping Up Initiative.

Launched in 2015 by the National Association of Counties (NACo), the Council of State Governments Justice Center, and the American Psychiatric Association Foundation, Stepping Up is a national movement designed to help counties reduce the number of people with mental illness in jails. Rather than accepting incarceration as the default response, the initiative encourages communities to examine their systems and build alternatives rooted in treatment and coordination.

Counties that participate in Stepping Up commit to several key strategies:

• Collecting accurate data about how many individuals with mental illness are entering their jail systems

• Improving screening and assessment so that mental health needs are identified early

• Expanding treatment options both inside and outside of jail

• Building stronger connections between courts, behavioral health providers, housing services, and community programs

• Tracking outcomes so communities can see whether reforms are actually reducing incarceration and improving health

As of recent years, more than 550 counties across the United States have joined the initiative, representing over half of the nation's population.

The goal is simple but powerful: reduce the number of people with serious mental illness cycling through local jails.

What makes Stepping Up important is that it recognizes something families like mine have known for years. The problem is not a lack of compassion. The problem is a lack of coordination.

When counties bring their systems together—courts, hospitals, law enforcement, housing, and behavioral health providers—they begin to see where people are falling through the cracks. Once those gaps become visible, communities can begin to fix them.

Programs like Stepping Up remind us that solutions already exist. They require leadership, collaboration, and the willingness to invest in approaches that prioritize treatment over incarceration.

These programs differ in structure but share common DNA: they are proactive, relationship-centered, and grounded in dignity.

What Innovation Requires

None of these programs started with perfect funding or full public support. They started because someone refused to accept failure as the only option.

Innovation happens when:

- People with lived experience are part of the design
- Systems are evaluated based on outcomes, not just intent
- Leaders are brave enough to pilot something new—even if it means making mistakes

We can't wait for federal reform to fix everything. Cities and counties have the power to lead, test, adapt, and scale what works.

The first time I heard about Miami's jail diversion model, I cried. Not because it was perfect—but because it existed. It meant that someone, somewhere, saw what we saw and decided to do something different.

We don't have to invent the solution from scratch. We can learn from what's working. We can replicate, adapt, and scale. Most importantly, we must act. Every day we delay innovation, someone else is lost to the very system we say we want to improve.

14

Policy with Purpose

If we know what works, why aren't we doing it?

That question has haunted me for years. After more than a decade navigating broken systems, I've come to believe that it's not a lack of ideas—it's a lack of alignment. Our policies are too often built for liability, not for lives. For headlines, not for healing. For budgets, not for people.

Policy doesn't have to be heartless. In fact, when done right, it can be one of the most compassionate tools we have.

What we need now is policy with purpose. Not more paperwork. Not more pilot programs that never scale. We need bold, data-informed decisions that center dignity, treatment, safety, and long-term outcomes—not temporary containment.

Redefining Crisis Response

1. Fund and Expand Mobile Crisis Teams
Every community needs a non-police mental health response option. Teams like CAHOOTS in Oregon and STAR in Denver

have demonstrated that mental health professionals can de-escalate many crises safely, respectfully, and often at a lower cost than traditional law enforcement responses.
Policy Action: Use federal Medicaid waivers and state grants to expand mobile crisis units statewide, with 24/7 coverage and regional dispatch.

2. Build and Sustain Crisis Stabilization Units (CSUs)
Instead of jail or the ER, people in crisis should have access to short-term facilities staffed by clinicians trained in psychiatric care. These units must be voluntary when possible and trauma-informed by design.
Policy Action: Require CSUs in every behavioral health region, and ensure they are integrated with outpatient and housing services.

Strengthening the Continuum of Care

3. Fully Fund Assisted Outpatient Treatment (AOT)
AOT works. Research consistently shows reductions in hospitalizations, arrests, and homelessness when programs are implemented with appropriate oversight and support. Sadly, in many states, AOT remains underfunded or inconsistently used due to lack of training, awareness, or political will.
Policy Action: Mandate state-level AOT infrastructure with consistent funding, data tracking, and family referral pathways.

4. Incentivize Assertive Community Treatment (ACT) Teams
ACT teams provide wraparound care to people with serious mental illness who often fall through the cracks. Yet many counties lack even one fully functioning team.
Policy Action: Offer state reimbursements for ACT team expan-

sion, and tie funding to client retention and engagement outcomes.

ACT works especially well because it recognizes an important truth: recovery is rarely linear. Relapses happen. Missed appointments happen. Moments of distrust happen. The goal is not perfection. The goal is sustained support through the instability.

Aligning Legal Protections with Clinical Reality

5. Modernize Civil Commitment Laws

The current "danger to self or others" standard is often reactive rather than preventive. In many situations, families and providers are forced to wait until a crisis escalates significantly before intervention becomes legally possible.

Policy Action: Consider adopting a "need for treatment" standard alongside current thresholds, using input from psychiatrists, legal experts, and caregivers.

Expanding the Definition of Crisis

Across the country, jurisdictions are beginning to recognize that the traditional legal threshold for intervention is too narrow to effectively protect individuals living with severe mental illness. Waiting until someone becomes actively dangerous often means waiting until the situation has already deteriorated beyond prevention.

Many communities are shifting toward language that recognizes functional decline, grave disability, or an individual in need of treatment.

Kentucky is one example of this shift.

Tim's Law, first enacted in 2017 and strengthened through

later amendments, established Assisted Outpatient Treatment pathways that allow courts to intervene when an individual with severe mental illness is deteriorating, even if they do not currently pose an immediate danger to themselves or others. Recent improvements broaden how a person's history of treatment non-adherence can be considered, emphasizing prevention of decline rather than waiting for crisis.

Kentucky law also recognizes self-neglect as a condition that may require intervention. Under Kentucky statute, an adult who cannot manage resources or carry out basic daily activities due to mental impairment may qualify as an individual in need of protective services.

Other states have adopted similar approaches.

In Arizona, involuntary treatment may be authorized if a person is considered "persistently or acutely disabled" or "gravely disabled," meaning they are unable to provide for their basic needs such as food, clothing, or shelter due to a mental disorder.

In California, Laura's Law allows courts to order outpatient treatment for individuals whose mental health condition is deteriorating and who have a history of hospitalization or incarceration linked to their illness.

These models reflect a broader shift away from the narrow "danger to self or others" standard that emerged from legal rulings in the 1970s. Increasingly, policymakers recognize that severe mental illness often first appears as functional decline, disorganization, or self-neglect, long before violence or suicide risk becomes apparent.

Allowing intervention earlier creates an opportunity to stabilize individuals before the situation escalates into tragedy.

6. Clarify HIPAA During Mental Health Crises

Families must be included in care—especially when the indi-

vidual is incapable of making informed decisions. Misinterpretation of HIPAA shouldn't cost people their lives.
Policy Action: Issue state and federal guidance on HIPAA exceptions during psychiatric emergencies, and provide staff training across health systems.

Resourcing Housing and Recovery

7. Prioritize Permanent Supportive Housing
Recovery is nearly impossible without housing. Supportive housing—where services are embedded—dramatically reduces recidivism and hospitalizations.
Policy Action: Allocate a set percentage of housing development funds toward supportive housing for people with SMI, and streamline voucher access.

A Progressive Pathway to Housing Stability

While many housing policies emphasize immediate placement into permanent housing, individuals with severe mental illness often benefit from a progressive pathway toward stability.

Housing First programs frequently operate most effectively when they include a continuum of supportive environments that allow individuals to stabilize and rebuild functioning over time.

These stages often include:

- Street outreach and drop-in engagement, where trust is built with individuals who may have experienced years of trauma or service failures.
- Temporary or safe haven housing, offering low-barrier environments with supportive staff where individuals can stabilize without pressure for immediate independence.

• Interim housing models, such as small community settings or private-room shelters, where individuals begin rebuilding daily routines and personal stability.

• Permanent supportive housing, where individuals live in their own apartment with voluntary services such as case management or ACT team support.

Without this progression, individuals who have endured chronic homelessness may be placed directly into independent housing without the stabilization and support necessary to sustain it. When housing programs fail under those conditions, the failure often reflects the system's design rather than the individual's capacity for recovery.

Effective housing policy recognizes that stability develops step by step.

8. Fund Peer Support and Family Navigation

Lived experience should be paid, professionalized, and embedded across systems—courts, hospitals, jails, shelters, and community programs.

Policy Action: Create state-funded peer support certification pathways and require at least one peer or family navigator in every behavioral health agency.

Focusing on Prevention, Not Just Containment

9. Invest in Early Identification and School-Based Services

Many young people show signs of mental illness long before a crisis. But due to stigma, cost, or lack of access, they go untreated for years.

Policy Action: Fund school-based mental health professionals, trauma screening, and family education partnerships as part of state prevention strategies.

• • •

10. Use Value-Based Reimbursement Models

Our current system rewards volume—not results. Providers are paid for visits, not outcomes. That must change.

Policy Action: Implement Medicaid waivers that pay providers for keeping clients housed, healthy, and out of the hospital or jail.

ADDITIONAL SYSTEM REFORMS WORTH CONSIDERING:

Workforce Development

One of the most pressing barriers to improving mental health services is the shortage of professionals entering the field. Behavioral health careers often require extensive training while offering compensation that struggles to compete with other professions requiring similar education.

Without meaningful investment in workforce development—including loan forgiveness programs, improved wages, and expanded training pathways—the system will continue to face staffing shortages that limit access to care.

Repealing the IMD Exclusion

Federal Medicaid policy still includes the Institution for Mental Diseases (IMD) Exclusion, which restricts Medicaid reimbursement for psychiatric facilities with more than sixteen beds serving adults between the ages of 21 and 64.

This decades-old policy limits the ability of states to build sufficient inpatient psychiatric capacity and continues to constrain access to needed treatment. Revisiting or repealing this exclusion could allow communities to expand treatment infrastructure and reduce reliance on jails and emergency rooms.

Rethinking Recidivism Metrics

Hospital systems often track recidivism rates, measuring how frequently patients return for hospitalization. While this metric may appear useful, it can unintentionally discourage hospitals from admitting individuals who require repeated stabilization.

If patients with severe illness are considered "frequent users," admitting them repeatedly increases recidivism statistics. This can create incentives to avoid admitting the very individuals who need care the most.

Measurement systems should reward treatment access and stabilization—not avoidance of complex patients.

Strengthening the 988 Crisis System

The 988 Suicide and Crisis Lifeline, launched nationally in 2022, has expanded access to mental health crisis support across the United States. By mid-2024, the system had handled millions of calls, texts, and chats nationwide.

Despite these improvements, several challenges remain.

Funding for 988 varies widely between states because only a limited number of states have established dedicated telecommunications fees similar to those that support the 911 emergency system. Without stable funding, crisis centers face staffing shortages and high turnover.

Public awareness also remains limited, with surveys suggesting that many Americans are still unfamiliar with the hotline number.

Operational challenges exist as well. Calls are currently routed based on a caller's area code, rather than their physical location, which can delay connection to local crisis resources when someone is traveling or calling from outside their home region.

Federal regulators are working toward implementing georouting technology intended to connect callers to the nearest crisis center based on location rather than phone number.

To reach its full potential, the 988 system must function as the front door to a comprehensive crisis continuum that includes mobile crisis teams, stabilization centers, and long-term follow-up care.

Training Legal Professionals

Judges, prosecutors, defense attorneys, and other legal professionals regularly encounter individuals living with severe mental illness. Expanding education and training in mental health conditions, diversion programs, and treatment options can help legal professionals respond more effectively and reduce unnecessary incarceration.

Where to Begin

Not every community can do everything at once, but every community can start. Here's a roadmap:

- Begin with crisis response (mobile teams, CSUs)
- Build toward care continuity (AOT, ACT, housing)
- Remove legal and bureaucratic barriers (HIPAA, commitment laws)
- Invest in what keeps people well—not just what controls them when they fall

If the moral case doesn't move lawmakers, the financial one should. Jail is expensive. Hospitalization is expensive. Doing nothing is often the most expensive option of all.

Policy is often portrayed as dry, distant, and technical. For families affected like my own, policy is intimate. It is whether my son receives care or punishment. Whether I get a call from a case manager or a coroner.

Every reform listed here has a face. A name. A family praying that this time, something will be different.

What we need now is the courage to build systems that reflect what we already know: recovery is possible, but not without help.

15

A Shared Safety Net

For years, I tried to be the safety net.

I called. I researched. I sat in meetings, took notes, showed up in court, begged caseworkers for updates, pleaded with doctors to intervene. I stayed up nights wondering where he was. I learned more than I ever wanted to know about medication, involuntary commitment, jail booking, and psychiatric evaluations. I've endured night terrors that scared me to death and long lasting PTSD.

I couldn't hold him up forever. No one person can.

That's the problem. In too many places, families are expected to carry the full weight of a broken system. If you don't have a parent with time, education, health, and resources—you fall. If your illness hits at just the wrong time—when a caseworker is out of office, carrying an unrealistic caseload, or when a program loses funding—you fall.

What we need is a system that catches people. Not sometimes. Not for a little while. Always.

What a Safety Net Really Means

A true safety net is not a single program. It is an interconnected web of support—available before, during, and after a crisis. It is the difference between surviving and slipping through the cracks.

It looks like:

- Someone answering the phone when a parent calls in fear.
- A bed available when someone needs stabilization.
- A place to live that doesn't disappear after 30 days.
- A care team that follows up, even when the person says no the first time.
- A doctor who sees a human being, not just a diagnosis.
- A judge who understands treatment is justice.

It also means no one is asked to do it all alone.

From Heroism to Infrastructure

We've built a system that relies on exceptional people to do impossible things.

- A police officer with CIT training who shows up instead of one who doesn't understand.
- A psychiatrist willing to dig deeper and find the real diagnosis.
- A parent with enough energy to go to every hearing and advocate through every setback.

These people matter. But we cannot depend on them to make up for what the system lacks. Hope should not hinge on whether a good cop or a good judge shows up on the right day.

We need infrastructure—not heroism.

When the Net Isn't There

My son has fallen through every gap imaginable. From discharge to street. From court to chaos. From ER to jail. I have watched him walk out of hospitals to the streets with no meds and no follow-up. I've received calls from jail staff saying, "He's here again," with no plan in place for anything different.

Each time I asked: Where is the net?

Why is there no consistent handoff from one system to the next? Why does the support stop the moment the crisis ends? Why do families have to become case managers just to hold their children together?

A Net Big Enough for All of Us

A shared safety net is built on the belief that mental illness is not a private problem. It's a public health reality—and a public responsibility.

- It's built when hospitals coordinate with housing providers before discharge.
- When schools screen early and refer without shame.
- When law enforcement defers to trained responders in psychiatric crises.
- When employers make space for recovery without penalty.
- When funding is stable, not pieced together with short-term grants.
- When families are included, not shut out.

A shared net lifts the burden from individual shoulders and places it where it belongs—on all of us, together.

What Shared Safety Would Have Looked Like for Jonathan

• A doctor recognizing bipolar disorder at nine—not years later.

• A psychologist and a psychiatrist working for the same organization collaborating together, rather than operating in silos, regarding their shared patient.

• Practitioners willing to consider each other's professional opinions—not disregarding them.

• A hospital keeping him for treatment when he was clearly unwell—not discharging him to the street.

• A judge using Tim's Law when it was passed—not waiting years for implementation.

• A care team that included me from the beginning—not only when things fell apart.

• A system that asked what he needed, not just what box he fit into.

That's what a safety net looks like.

We cannot prevent every crisis, but we can prevent the pattern of abandonment that follows them.

The opposite of falling through the cracks is being caught—with compassion, with continuity, with care that doesn't depend on luck or privilege.

This is what we owe one another.

We've spent decades building systems that punish, isolate, and blame. It's time to build one that holds. Because when we build a shared safety net, we don't just protect people with serious mental illness—we protect our collective humanity.

Part III

What does it take to lead change—in real time, with real people, in real communities?

16

From Caregiver to Advocate

I didn't become an advocate because I had extra time. I became one because I didn't have a choice.

When your child is arrested instead of treated…

When you watch them spiral through hospitals and courtrooms…

When no one answers the phone, and no one takes responsibility…

You either speak up—or you go under. You fight—or melt into a puddle.

I used to think advocacy meant standing at a podium or sitting on a board. And sometimes it does. But more often, it looks like emailing the school after another suspension. Sitting in court. Organizing paperwork for the sixth intake. Keeping a journal of symptoms. Learning laws you never thought you'd need to understand.

It's not glamorous. *It's survival.*

Over time, something changes. You start to see patterns. You realize that your story is not just personal—it's political. You begin to want more than a temporary fix. You want transformation. That's when caregiving begins to shift into advocacy.

When Advocacy Finds You

I didn't ask for this path. But I couldn't ignore it.

After years of watching my son fall through every gap, I realized: If I kept quiet, I was complicit. Not in his suffering, but in the silence that allowed it to continue for others.

So I started showing up. To community forums. To city council meetings. To news interviews. I spoke not only for my son—but for the thousands of families whose stories mirror ours.

It was hard. I was still in the thick of it. I wasn't healed. But I had something to say. Sometimes, that's all it takes.

The Cost of Always Being "On"

Let me be clear: advocacy can be exhausting.

You're showing up for your loved one. You're explaining the system to people who have never lived it. You're writing emails while grieving, making calls while managing symptoms, attending hearings after sleepless nights.

And sometimes, you're doing it while people question your motives. While professionals dismiss your insights. While your own friends stop asking how you're doing.

This work takes a toll—physically, emotionally, spiritually. I've had to learn (and re-learn) that I cannot be everything for everyone. I have walked straight into burnout more than once.

Staying in the Work Without Losing Yourself

Here's what I've learned about doing this work sustainably:

- Rest is not weakness. You can step back without giving up. Advocacy is a relay, not a solo sprint.
- You don't have to do it all. Choose the lane that gives you life—or at least doesn't drain it. Is it writing? Organizing? Testifying? Supporting others?
- Build a circle. Find others who get it. You need people who can hear the rage and the grief without turning away.
- Protect your story. You don't owe anyone the most painful parts. Share what you're ready to carry in public.
- Celebrate the wins. Even the small ones. Especially the small ones.

When the System Calls You In

Eventually, people started to ask me to share what I knew.

They asked me to consult on policy proposals, speak at conferences, and train providers. Suddenly, the same systems that once excluded me were asking for my insight.

At first, I didn't know if I belonged. I wasn't a clinician. I wasn't a policymaker. But I was the one who lived it. And that lived experience had value they couldn't find anywhere else.

You may find the same. You may be called into rooms you never expected—because your perspective is the missing piece.

Say yes when you're ready. Say no when you're not. But know this: You belong there.

The Power of Showing Up Again and Again

I've learned that advocacy is not always loud.

Sometimes it's quiet persistence.

It's calling again.

Showing up again.

Writing it down.

Speaking the truth when it's easier to stay polite.

Refusing to normalize the unacceptable.

Not waiting for permission to share your insights.

Every time you do that, you're chipping away at the wall. Every time you ask the hard question or bring lived reality into the room, you are creating space for something better.

You don't need to be perfect to be powerful. You don't need to be healed to speak. You just need to care enough to keep showing up—even when it's hard.

Caregiving is advocacy. Advocacy is leadership. Leadership doesn't always look like a megaphone. Sometimes it looks like love, stubborn and steady.

You've been doing more than surviving. You've been lighting a path.

17

Local Action That Matters

The first time I spoke at a CIT training for a room full of law enforcement officers, I thought, *What am I doing here?*

What could I possibly have to say to these officers that would help them in their jobs? They were professionals charged with enforcing the law. What did I know? How were they going to find me credible? Surely they already knew this material. What could I add that they didn't already understand?

I had so many fears about talking to them.

I was exhausted. Still fighting fires at home. Still catching my breath from the last crisis. But I knew I had something to say. Not just as a mother, but as a witness. I had seen what happens when systems don't talk to each other. When budgets go to punishment instead of prevention. When no one takes ownership—and everyone suffers.

So I stood up. And I spoke. And someone listened.

To my shock and surprise, it turned out I had a great deal to share—and they wanted to hear it. They were engaged. They wanted to know more from a lived-experience perspective. They wanted to better understand mental illness and the people living with it.

That was the beginning of something. Not overnight change. But a shift. A door opening. A sense that maybe, just maybe, what we do at the local level can matter.

Why Local Change Is Often the Most Powerful

It's easy to get overwhelmed by federal policy. To feel like nothing you do can move the needle. But here's the truth: some of the most meaningful reforms start close to home.

- A county judge launches a mental health docket.
- A sheriff diverts funding toward reentry support.
- A school district hires a trauma-informed social worker.
- A hospital shifts discharge planning to include housing partners.

None of these changes required an act of Congress. They started because someone saw a gap and said, "We can do better here."

You can be that someone.

The Systems Closest to You

Here's where local advocacy can make a real difference:

1. Court Systems
Advocating for behavioral health dockets, court-ordered treatment options, and judges trained in mental illness.
Real impact: Fewer jail sentences. More treatment alternatives.

2. Jails & Law Enforcement

Pushing for CIT training, jail diversion programs, and better mental health screening.
Real impact: Reduced arrests and safer outcomes during crises.

3. Schools
Encouraging early mental health screening, staff training, and crisis response protocols.
Real impact: Earlier intervention and reduced criminalization of behavior.

4. Hospitals
Demanding better discharge coordination, follow-up care, and collaboration with housing and outpatient providers.
Real impact: Fewer readmissions and better continuity of care.

5. City & County Budgets
Attending budget hearings. Asking how mental health funding is allocated.
Real impact: Money shifts from emergency response toward prevention.

6. Local Advocacy Groups
Groups like the National Alliance on Mental Illness (NAMI) are already in the fight. Join them. Your voice, added to theirs, truly matters.

How to Start Where You Are

You don't need a policy degree. You need proximity and persistence.

- Show up. Attend public meetings. Speak during open comment.

• Get on the agenda. Ask to present your story or a proposed solution.

• Ask questions. Where does our mental health funding go? How many crisis beds do we have? What is our crisis response protocol?

• Build relationships. Find allies in city departments, nonprofits, law enforcement, healthcare systems, and faith communities.

• Connect the dots. Help leaders understand how disconnected systems harm real people.

The goal isn't to be an expert in everything. It's to bring human experience into decision-making.

When Local Work Leads to Big Change

In Kentucky, we didn't wait for a national directive. We started with what we had.

A group of cross-disciplinary professionals, alongside individuals with lived experience, came together to collaborate, brainstorm, and share knowledge from many perspectives.

Eventually, Tim's Law was conceived, refined, and enacted. At first it wasn't perfect—but it mattered. It took years of work, advocacy, and collaboration before implementation began to take shape. It showed what was possible.

I've watched other communities take meaningful steps:

• Miami-Dade County, Florida: Expanded diversion programs connecting people with serious mental illness to treatment instead of jail.

• San Antonio and Bexar County, Texas: Built coordinated crisis response systems and expanded diversion efforts through cross-system collaboration.

• Communities across the country: Expanded CIT training, mental health courts, crisis stabilization services, and partnerships between behavioral health and public safety agencies.

These weren't federal mandates. They were local leaders who listened—and acted.

You Are Not "Just a Parent"

Sometimes when I speak at local meetings, I still hear that voice in my head: *You're just a mom.*

But that voice is wrong.

I'm not just anything.

I'm someone who knows the system inside and out—not because I studied it in a classroom, but because I survived it. And that knowledge is powerful.

So is yours.

Local work isn't flashy. It's slow. It's messy. It's showing up to yet another meeting when you'd rather be anywhere else.

But it's where hearts change.

Where policies begin.

Where momentum grows.

You don't have to change the whole system.

Just your corner of it.

That's enough.

They weren't elected officials. They were local leaders who listened and acted.

You Are Not "Just a Parent"

Sometimes, when I speak at a local meeting, I still hear that voice in my head: *She's just a mom.*

But that voice is wrong.

I'm not just anything.

I'm someone who knows the system inside and out—not because I studied it in a classroom, but because I survived it. And that knowledge is powerful.

So is yours.

Local work isn't flashy. It's slow. It's messy. It's showing up to yet another meeting when you'd rather be anywhere else.

But it's where lives change.

Where policies begin.

Where momentum grows.

You don't have to change the whole system.

Just your corner of it.

That's enough.

18

Leadership from the Margins

For a long time, I didn't see myself as a leader. I saw myself as a mother in survival mode—fighting fires, managing symptoms, filling out paperwork, asking questions no one could answer.

Over time, something shifted. I realized that I wasn't just reacting. I was leading. I was mapping out gaps in the system. I was helping professionals see what they'd missed. I was building bridges between the people experiencing the crisis and those who claimed to solve it. And I was doing it without a title, without a salary, without an invitation.

This is what leadership from the margins looks like.

The People Closest to the Problem Hold the Keys

When we talk about leadership in mental health reform, we often picture policymakers, clinicians, or executives. But those closest to the issue—families, peers, survivors, direct care workers—carry a wisdom no textbook can teach.

You've lived the chaos.

You've endured the silence.

You've built workarounds because the official system had nothing to offer.

That's not a limitation. That's lived expertise.

The Table Isn't Always Built for Us

You may have been told, directly or indirectly, that you don't belong in policy meetings, budget discussions, or leadership circles. I've been there. I've sat through rooms where people used acronyms I'd never heard, where decisions were made without anyone who had actually experienced the system.

At first, I waited for someone to invite me to the table.

Eventually, I realized: if the table wasn't built for us, we have the right to build our own. Often, when we do, others come. Because they're hungry for something real.

Claiming Leadership Without Permission

You don't need credentials to lead. What you need is clarity—and community.

Here's what leadership from the margins can look like:

• A mother testifying before the school board about seclusion policies.

• A person with schizophrenia training police officers on how to respond with dignity.

• A caregiver helping another family fill out Medicaid forms.

• A formerly incarcerated individual teaching reentry staff what actually works.

• A peer mentor leading support groups that therapists can't replicate.

Leadership is influence. And if you're helping shift mindsets, practices, or policies—even in small ways—you're already leading.

Barriers Are Real—But Not Final

It's important to name the obstacles:

• Gatekeeping: Some spaces still resist people with lived experience.

• Burnout: It's hard to lead when you're still living the trauma.

• Stigma: People may minimize or dismiss your story.

• Tokenism: You're invited to speak but not to shape decisions.

Here's the truth: the most transformative change often begins with people the system least expects. We're not here because it's easy. We're here because it's necessary.

When we show up—even tired, even angry, even grieving—we bring something that can't be replicated: the truth.

Ways to Lead From Where You Are

You don't have to wait until everything is fixed in your own life to begin.

• Advocate: Share your story with policymakers, providers, and media.

• Organize: Bring together other families or peers. Start small. Build power together.

• Educate: Train professionals on what it's like to live through the system.

• Collaborate: Offer to consult on task forces, advisory boards, or planning teams.

• Create: Write op-eds. Build resource guides. Host webinars. Build new models.

You don't need a megaphone. Just a willingness to speak up, and the courage to keep going.

Redefining What Leadership Looks Like

For too long, leadership has looked like power suits, policy degrees, and clean hands. But real leadership—the kind that changes lives—often looks like:

- Wrinkled intake forms stuffed in a purse.
- A notepad full of court dates.
- A quiet voice that trembles—but doesn't stop.
- Eyes that have seen too much—and still look forward.

That's the kind of leadership I trust.

They may never give you a nameplate. You may never get a title. But if you're showing up, telling the truth, refusing to let silence have the last word—You're already doing the work of transformation. If enough of us lead from the margins, eventually the margins move.

19

Building the Future We Deserve

When I look back at the last twelve years, what I see is a family who refused to give up—no matter how many times the system failed us.

I see late-night ER visits, unanswered voicemails, courtrooms, breakdowns, and long walks across the city searching for my son. But I also see resilience. I see the people who listened. The social worker who went the extra mile. The judge who saw my son as more than a case number. The community partners who finally said, "Let's do this differently." It's from that place—not bitterness, but hard-earned clarity—that I say this:

We deserve better.

And not just my family.

Every family. Every individual struggling with mental illness deserves a future that isn't shaped by fear, isolation, or incarceration.

It Starts With What We Believe Is Possible

We will never build a better system if we believe that what we have is the best we can do.

When we stop asking why there aren't enough beds, why families aren't supported, why hospitals won't admit individuals in crisis and in need of help**, or why they discharge people without meaningful follow-up,** we stop imagining. When we stop imagining, we stop building.

But I've seen what's possible when we do imagine something different:

• A city where mobile crisis teams respond instead of police

• A community center with peer specialists and respite beds

• A school that doesn't call 911 first, but calls a trauma-informed team

• A court that asks, "What treatment does this person need?" instead of "What charge fits?"

• A drop-in center for homeless individuals to gather when shelters are closed, where they can do laundry, store belongings in lockers, and connect with social service professionals

• A 23-hour stabilization unit instead of a jail cell

• An urgent care designed specifically for mental health

• A system where there is "no wrong door" for accessing services

• A system where no one leaves without a treatment plan

• An intake process that is compassionate, accessible, and free from judgment

These aren't dreams. They exist. Just not everywhere. Not for everyone.

Yet.

What a Just System Could Look Like

A future that honors people with serious mental illness would include:

• Early intervention: Schools and pediatricians trained to recognize and respond to early symptoms

• Accessible treatment: Walk-in clinics, same-day psychiatric appointments, and culturally responsive providers

• Supportive housing: No one discharged from care to the street

• Crisis response without criminalization: Mental health professionals as first responders

• Family engagement: HIPAA policies that allow collaboration, not secrecy

• Care that doesn't expire: Ongoing, relationship-based support—not 30-day limits

That's the system I want to see. That's the one we must demand.

Real Change Needs Everyone

Policy experts can write laws. But caregivers like me can tell you if those laws work.

Clinicians can diagnose and treat—but peers can help people stay connected.

Officials can set budgets—but community voices can help identify what is worth funding.

Real change is not top-down. It's relational. It's collaborative. It's built by people who are willing to listen—and even more willing to learn.

The Role of Lived Experience in System Design

We cannot build a better future without the insights of those who have survived the worst of the current one.

Whether it's families like mine, individuals in recovery, or frontline case managers, those voices must be in the room—not just telling their stories, but shaping the solutions.

Hire them. Invite them. Fund them. Let them co-lead. Not because it's trendy. But because it's necessary.

From Scarcity to Vision

One of the biggest barriers to change is the belief that there isn't enough:

Not enough money.

Not enough staff.

Not enough time.

But what if we flipped the question?

What is the cost of continuing not to act?

What are we losing every year we delay?

- Human life
- Family stability
- Community trust
- Financial resources
- Hope

We don't need to spend more. We need to spend more intentionally.

We need to spend with purpose. With values. With vision.

I've spent more than a decade inside the mess—trying to navigate systems that weren't designed for families like mine. But I've also witnessed sparks of change. I've seen leaders grow brave.

Communities come together. Young people recover. Judges rewrite what justice looks like.

That is what keeps me going.

We're not just asking for services. We're asking for dignity. We're asking for healing. We're asking for a future where people with serious mental illness are not feared, ignored, or locked away—but seen, supported, and valued.

We're not broken. The system is.

Let's build something better.

Part IV

20

Safety Without Shackles

One of the most terrifying realities for families navigating severe mental illness is knowing that a mental health crisis often begins with a call for help—but ends with handcuffs.

For years, families like mine have faced an impossible decision. Call 911 and risk escalation, arrest, or even violence… or do nothing and hope the situation does not spiral further.

No family should have to make that choice.

When Jonathan was in psychosis, what he needed most was stabilization, compassion, and trained mental health intervention. Too often, what arrived instead were police officers with limited psychiatric training responding to situations rooted in fear, confusion, hallucinations, and neurological impairment.

Law enforcement officers are asked to carry responsibilities they were never designed to hold. Many do their best within impossible circumstances. Yet mental illness is a healthcare issue, not a criminal justice issue.

The reality is simple: people in crisis need care—not cuffs.

Expanding the Crisis Response Toolbox

In many communities, first responders effectively have only two options available during a psychiatric crisis:

- Jail
- Emergency room hospitalization

Neither option was designed to provide long-term psychiatric stabilization.

What if communities created eight or ten options instead?

What if first responders could connect individuals to:

- Mobile crisis teams
- Crisis stabilization units
- Psychiatric urgent care centers
- Peer respite programs
- Behavioral health drop-off centers
- Short-term observation units
- Transitional respite housing
- Community mental health navigators
- Telepsychiatry consultation
- Specialized behavioral health transportation teams

That kind of system changes outcomes.

Instead of asking, "Where can we take this person?" communities begin asking, "What does this person actually need?"

Mobile Crisis Teams

Programs such as CAHOOTS in Eugene, Oregon, and STAR in Denver, Colorado, have demonstrated that mental health professionals can safely respond to many psychiatric crises without relying primarily on law enforcement.

These teams often include clinicians, paramedics, social workers, or peer support specialists trained specifically in de-escalation and psychiatric response.

The results are significant:

- Reduced arrests
- Reduced use of force
- Lower emergency room utilization
- Lower public safety costs
- Increased connection to treatment

Many calls traditionally routed to police involve homelessness, confusion, suicidal ideation, substance use, or psychiatric distress rather than violent criminal activity.

Communities that invest in mobile crisis infrastructure create safer outcomes for everyone involved.

Why Police Should Not Be the Default Response

Police officers are trained to secure scenes and respond quickly to threats. Psychiatric crises often require the opposite approach:

- Slowing down
- Reducing stimulation
- Building trust
- Using relational communication

For someone experiencing psychosis, uniforms, loud commands, flashing lights, or physical restraint can intensify paranoia and fear.

A frightened person may appear resistant or aggressive when they are actually disoriented.

This creates danger for everyone involved.

According to the Treatment Advocacy Center, individuals with untreated severe mental illness are significantly more likely to experience fatal encounters with law enforcement during psychiatric crises.

Many of those tragedies began with someone calling for help.

Communities must stop treating law enforcement as the primary mental health infrastructure.

Behavioral Health Dockets and Jail Diversion

Some communities are beginning to rethink the revolving door between jails and psychiatric crises.

Behavioral health dockets, mental health courts, and diversion programs recognize that many individuals entering the justice system are struggling with untreated illness rather than criminal intent.

These programs redirect individuals toward:

- Treatment
- Medication support
- Case management
- Housing
- Accountability structures
- Recovery services

Instead of repeatedly cycling individuals through arrest and release, diversion programs focus on stabilization and long-term outcomes.

Programs across Ohio, Texas, Florida, and Kentucky have shown measurable reductions in incarceration rates and emergency system utilization when diversion systems are properly funded and coordinated.

Crisis Stabilization Units

Emergency rooms were never intended to function as long-term psychiatric holding centers. Yet across the country, individuals in crisis spend hours—or even days—waiting in overstimulating emergency departments for psychiatric placement.

Crisis Stabilization Units provide another option.

These units offer short-term psychiatric observation and treatment in calmer, clinically appropriate settings designed specifically for behavioral health crises.

Individuals can often:

- Receive medication stabilization
- Connect with case management
- Avoid incarceration
- Avoid unnecessary hospitalization
- Transition directly into outpatient services

For many communities, CSUs create a desperately needed middle ground between jail and inpatient hospitalization.

What Your Community Can Do Next

Communities do not need to solve every problem overnight. Meaningful reform often begins with a few strategic changes.

Cities and counties can:

- Expand mobile crisis teams
- Establish behavioral health drop-off centers
- Invest in crisis stabilization units
- Create behavioral health dockets
- Integrate peer support into emergency response
- Train dispatchers to identify psychiatric crises
- Build partnerships between hospitals, courts, law enforcement, and community providers

Every additional option reduces the likelihood that jail becomes the default response.

For too long, communities have expected jails and emergency rooms to absorb the consequences of untreated mental illness.

That approach has failed families, overwhelmed systems, and traumatized individuals already struggling to survive.

Safety should never require criminalization.

The measure of a compassionate society is not how quickly it punishes people in crisis. The measure is whether it creates pathways toward healing before punishment becomes the only response left.

People in crisis need care—not cuffs.

21

Investing in What Works

One of the most frustrating realities families face is realizing that the money already exists. The problem is not always a lack of funding. The problem is where that funding goes.

For years I watched communities spend enormous amounts of money responding to psychiatric crises after they exploded, while investing very little in preventing those crises from happening in the first place.

Jonathan could spend days in an emergency room waiting for psychiatric placement. He could be arrested repeatedly and cycle through jails, hospitals, shelters, and courtrooms. Every part of that process cost money. Ambulances cost money. Police response costs money. Emergency room boarding costs money. Jail stays cost money.

Still, when families ask for housing support, intensive outpatient services, peer support, ACT teams, or long-term stabilization programs, we are often told the same thing.

"There isn't enough funding."

The contradiction becomes impossible to ignore.

Our systems spend extraordinary amounts of money managing collapse while investing far less in recovery.

What We Fund vs. What Works

Much of the current behavioral health funding structure rewards volume rather than outcomes.

Hospitals are reimbursed for admissions. Emergency systems are funded for crisis response. Jails receive budgets tied to incarceration capacity. Short-term stabilization often receives priority over long-term recovery.

Meanwhile, many of the services proven to reduce crisis remain underfunded:

- Supportive housing
- Peer support
- ACT teams
- Early intervention
- Long-term community treatment
- Family navigation
- Mobile crisis response

The result is a system that pays heavily for failure while struggling to sustain success.

Research from counties participating in the Stepping Up Initiative demonstrates that communities investing in diversion programs, coordinated care, and behavioral health treatment often reduce incarceration rates while lowering public costs over time.

The evidence already exists. Communities simply need the willingness to invest differently.

Following the Money

If we truly want to understand what society values, we should follow the money.

Many counties spend significantly more on incarceration than on community mental health services. Psychiatric crises frequently end inside systems never designed to treat mental illness effectively.

A jail bed may cost hundreds of dollars per night. Emergency room boarding can cost even more. Repeated hospitalizations, arrests, and police interventions quickly consume public resources.

Supportive housing, peer support, and outpatient treatment are often far less expensive over time.

The challenge is that prevention rarely creates dramatic headlines. Successful stabilization often looks quiet. A person remains housed. A crisis never occurs. A family sleeps through the night without calling 911.

Those successes rarely attract attention, yet they represent the very outcomes communities claim to want.

Value-Based Funding

The healthcare system increasingly talks about "value-based care," meaning providers are rewarded for improved outcomes rather than simply the number of services delivered.

Mental health systems should move in the same direction.

Imagine if providers were rewarded for:

- Reducing homelessness
- Preventing incarceration
- Improving treatment engagement
- Keeping individuals connected to care
- Reducing psychiatric crises over time

That approach would fundamentally change how systems prioritize services.

Right now many organizations survive financially by responding to repeated crises. A healthier system would reward communities for preventing those crises in the first place.

Federal Innovation and Medicaid Reform

Federal policy plays an enormous role in shaping local mental health systems.

Medicaid waivers and federal innovation grants give states opportunities to redesign behavioral health infrastructure, yet many communities struggle to fully utilize those tools.

Policies such as the IMD Exclusion, which limits Medicaid reimbursement for larger psychiatric facilities, continue to restrict treatment capacity nationwide. Workforce shortages create additional barriers. Many mental health professionals leave the field due to burnout, unsustainable caseloads, and inadequate compensation.

At the same time, communities often lack sufficient reimbursement for outreach services, peer support, housing coordination, and long-term stabilization work.

These gaps create predictable consequences:

- Overcrowded emergency rooms
- Repeated incarceration
- Homelessness
- Fragmented treatment
- Revolving-door care

The system continues paying for instability instead of investing in continuity.

The Cost of Doing Nothing

Families understand the hidden costs better than any spreadsheet can capture.

We lose jobs while caring for loved ones in crisis. Savings disappear paying for private treatment, attorneys, transportation, hotels near hospitals, and missed work. Relationships fracture under stress. Siblings grow up inside chronic uncertainty.

Communities absorb those costs as well.

Public safety systems become overwhelmed. Emergency departments fill beyond capacity. Homelessness rises. Jails become psychiatric holding facilities. Police officers shoulder responsibilities that belong within healthcare systems.

Doing nothing is not cheaper.

Doing nothing simply spreads the cost across families, emergency systems, courts, hospitals, and communities while human suffering grows.

Building Systems That Reflect Our Values

Communities already know what works.

Research consistently supports:

- ACT teams
- Supportive housing
- Early intervention
- Coordinated care
- Mobile crisis response
- Peer support
- Diversion programs
- Long-term outpatient treatment

The challenge is no longer identifying effective strategies. The challenge is building the political and financial will to prioritize them.

A society's values are reflected not only in speeches or mission statements, but in budgets.

Budgets reveal what we are truly willing to protect.

For too long, mental health systems have been funded around containment instead of recovery.

Families like mine have watched communities spend enormous amounts of money responding to psychiatric collapse while investing far less in preventing it.

That imbalance must change.

If we want fewer arrests, we must invest in treatment. If we want fewer psychiatric crises, we must invest in stability. If we want healthier communities, we must fund the services that help people remain connected, housed, and supported.

If we want different outcomes, we must invest in the things that make those outcomes possible.

If you want to see what we value, follow the money.

22

Centering Lived Expertise

One of the greatest weaknesses within many mental health systems is that the people most affected by those systems are often the least included in designing them.

Families sit in waiting rooms for years learning how fragmented systems function. Individuals living with serious mental illness navigate barriers that many policymakers and administrators never personally experience. Peer specialists understand recovery in ways textbooks alone cannot teach.

Still, too many decisions are made without those voices in the room.

Systems built without lived expertise often miss the realities families encounter every day.

The Knowledge That Comes From Survival

There is a difference between studying a system and surviving one.

Families learn quickly how difficult it can be to navigate

mental health care. We learn which emergency rooms avoid psychiatric admissions. We learn how to communicate with providers during crises. We learn what happens when someone loses housing, stops medication, or disappears into psychosis.

That knowledge is not theoretical.

It is earned through sleepless nights, failed phone calls, court hearings, emergency transports, and moments of fear most people never witness.

People living with serious mental illness carry expertise as well. They understand what treatment feels like from the inside. They know which interactions build trust and which create shame. They know how systems succeed and where they fail.

Communities become stronger when those perspectives shape decision-making.

"Nothing About Us Without Us"

The disability rights movement introduced a phrase that remains deeply important in mental health reform:

"Nothing about us without us."

The meaning is simple. Policies should not be created for people without including the people directly affected by those policies.

That principle matters in:

- hospitals
- courts
- housing systems
- crisis response planning
- legislative reform
- treatment program design

Too often individuals with lived experience are invited to share emotional stories while professionals retain decision-making power. Real inclusion requires more than symbolic participation.

People with lived experience should help lead systems—not simply appear beside them.

Paying People for Their Expertise

One of the most meaningful shifts happening in behavioral health is the growing recognition of peer support specialists and family navigators.

For years, caregivers and individuals in recovery provided guidance informally:

- helping families understand the system
- explaining treatment options
- supporting people through crisis
- assisting with housing and benefits
- building trust where systems had failed

Many communities now recognize that this work is valuable professional expertise.

Peer specialists can often connect with individuals in ways traditional providers cannot. Shared experience creates credibility. Trust grows differently when someone says, "I have lived this too."

That expertise deserves compensation, training, and leadership opportunities.

Advisory Boards and Co-Led Systems

Mental health systems improve when they create meaningful feedback loops with families and individuals directly affected by care.

Advisory boards that include:

- caregivers
- individuals in recovery
- peer specialists

- direct service workers
- housing advocates
- community members

can often identify problems long before they appear in formal reports or administrative reviews.

Co-led training between clinicians and people with lived experience can also transform professional culture. Providers gain a deeper understanding of how policies and interactions affect individuals outside clinical settings.

These collaborations build systems that feel more human, more responsive, and more effective.

Rethinking HIPAA

HIPAA was designed to protect privacy. In many situations, it serves an important purpose.

At the same time, families navigating severe mental illness often experience HIPAA as a wall instead of a safeguard.

Caregivers may be excluded from conversations even when they:

- provide housing
- coordinate appointments
- transport loved ones to treatment
- manage medications
- monitor symptoms
- respond during crises

Many providers misunderstand what HIPAA actually allows during psychiatric emergencies. Families are frequently denied basic communication that could improve safety and continuity of care.

Mental health systems must find ways to balance autonomy with collaboration.

Privacy protections should not prevent life-saving partnership.

How Systems Change When Lived Experience Leads

Communities that integrate lived expertise often develop more compassionate and practical approaches.

Programs shaped by individuals with direct experience tend to:

- reduce stigma
- improve engagement
- increase trust
- identify service gaps earlier
- strengthen continuity of care
- improve long-term outcomes

People who have survived psychiatric crisis frequently recognize barriers professionals overlook.

They know what it feels like to:

- fear hospitalization
- lose housing
- avoid treatment
- distrust systems
- experience psychosis
- navigate hopelessness

That perspective matters.

It is not merely an emotional contribution to reform. It is a source of practical knowledge that can improve how systems function.

Mental health systems grow stronger when they stop viewing lived experience as secondary to professional expertise.

Families, peers, and individuals in recovery carry insights that cannot be learned through policy manuals alone.

The goal is not to replace clinical expertise. The goal is partnership.

Healing becomes more possible when systems listen carefully to the people who know the terrain firsthand.

The system gets smarter when we listen to those who survived it.

23

When They Don't Believe They're Sick

UNDERSTANDING ANOSOGNOSIA, LEAP, AND THE POWER OF CONNECTION

One of the most painful realities families face is realizing that love alone cannot convince someone they are ill.

For years, I believed that if I could just explain things clearly enough, Jonathan would eventually understand what was happening to him. I tried logic. I tried pleading. I tried facts, tears, arguments, ultimatums, encouragement, and fear. I carried medical records into conversations like evidence I hoped would finally persuade him.

None of it worked.

The harder I pushed, the more distant he became.

At the time, I misunderstood what I was seeing. I thought Jonathan was denying his illness. I thought he was refusing reality.

What I eventually learned changed everything.

Many individuals living with severe mental illness experience a neurological symptom called anosognosia, a condition that impairs a person's ability to recognize or accurately understand that they are experiencing a mental illness. This is not stubbornness. It is not manipulation. It is not laziness or rebellion.

The brain genuinely cannot accurately perceive the illness.

That understanding reframed years of conflict inside our family.

The Cruel Paradox of Severe Mental Illness

One of the cruelest aspects of psychosis is that the illness itself can damage the very insight needed to seek treatment.

A person may clearly see that everyone else is wrong while remaining unable to recognize their own disorganized thinking, paranoia, hallucinations, or delusions. To them, their experiences feel completely real.

Trying to argue someone out of psychosis often creates greater distrust. Family members become part of the perceived threat. Conversations escalate. Relationships fracture under the weight of repeated attempts to force insight.

Many caregivers live trapped in that exhausting cycle.

We plead for treatment while the person we love insists nothing is wrong.

The emotional toll becomes enormous.

Parents begin questioning themselves. Siblings withdraw. Marriages strain under chronic crisis. Fear quietly settles into the home.

What families often need most in those moments is not another argument strategy. They need a different way to communicate.

Discovering LEAP

Dr. Xavier Amador developed a communication framework known as LEAP after his own experiences with a family member living with schizophrenia.

LEAP stands for:

- *Listen*
- *Empathize*
- *Agree*
- *Partner*

The approach is deceptively simple, yet profoundly difficult.

Instead of trying to force someone to accept a diagnosis, LEAP teaches families and providers to begin by building trust.

Listening becomes more important than correcting. Empathy becomes more effective than confrontation.

This does not mean pretending delusions are real. It means recognizing that the emotional experience underneath them is real.

If someone says they are terrified, the fear itself deserves acknowledgment even if the belief causing it is inaccurate.

That distinction matters.

Listening Before Correcting

One of the hardest lessons for caregivers is learning that being right is not always the same thing as being effective.

When Jonathan was in psychosis, my instinct was often to immediately challenge irrational thinking. I wanted to pull him back into reality as quickly as possible.

What usually happened instead was escalation.

The more intensely I argued, the more frightened and defensive he became.

LEAP encouraged something entirely different.

Instead of saying:

"That isn't true."

The approach encourages responses such as:

"That sounds frightening."

"I can see this feels very real to you."

"Help me understand what you're experiencing."

Those small shifts reduce defensiveness. Trust begins to grow when individuals feel heard rather than corrected.

Connection becomes possible again.

Agreement Without Surrender

One of the greatest misconceptions about LEAP is that empathy means agreeing with delusions.

It does not.

Families can agree on shared goals without agreeing on distorted beliefs.

For example, Jonathan and I might disagree about whether he was experiencing psychosis. At the same time, we could agree that:

- he wanted to feel safer
- he wanted less anxiety
- he wanted housing
- he wanted sleep
- he wanted fewer conflicts

Shared goals create openings for treatment conversations.

Partnership becomes more achievable when discussions focus on improving quality of life rather than forcing insight.

The Importance of Trust

Trust is one of the most fragile and essential elements in mental health care.

Individuals living with psychosis often experience repeated trauma within systems:

- involuntary hospitalization
- forced medication
- incarceration

• frightening police encounters
• restraint
• social rejection

Distrust develops naturally under those conditions.

Families carry trauma too. Many caregivers live in a constant state of hypervigilance, anticipating the next crisis, arrest, hospitalization, or disappearance.

LEAP does not erase that trauma. It does offer a framework that reduces conflict and preserves connection.

Sometimes maintaining connection is the most important intervention available.

What Systems Could Learn From LEAP

Mental health systems frequently prioritize compliance over relationship.

Appointments become transactional. Crisis response becomes procedural. Individuals are often treated as problems to stabilize rather than people trying to survive frightening neurological experiences.

LEAP offers a different model.

It reminds providers, families, law enforcement officers, judges, and policymakers that trust matters. People are more likely to engage in treatment when they feel respected, heard, and emotionally safe.

Training professionals in LEAP-informed communication could help improve:

• crisis response
• treatment engagement
• family relationships
• continuity of care
• long-term outcomes

Relational approaches are not soft alternatives to treatment. They are often the bridge that makes treatment possible.

For years I believed my job was to convince Jonathan that he was sick.

Over time I realized my first responsibility was preserving enough trust that he would continue allowing me into his world.

That shift changed the way I communicated, listened, and responded during crisis.

Anosognosia taught me that insight cannot always be forced. LEAP taught me that connection still can.

People living with severe mental illness do not only need medication, housing, and services. They need relationships strong enough to survive fear, confusion, and disconnection.

Healing often begins there.

24

Accountability Without Blame

One of the greatest obstacles to meaningful reform is the fear that accountability automatically means punishment.

Hospitals fear liability. Providers fear lawsuits. Law enforcement agencies fear criticism. Administrators fear bad publicity. Politicians fear public backlash.

As a result, systems often become defensive rather than reflective.

Families know this pattern well.

A psychiatric discharge goes badly. A crisis escalates. Someone is harmed. A preventable tragedy unfolds. Instead of openly examining what failed, institutions often retreat into silence, legal language, and bureaucratic protection.

Records become difficult to access. Questions go unanswered. Responsibility scatters across disconnected systems until no one appears accountable at all.

The result is not trust.

The result is exhaustion and grief layered on top of trauma.

Systems Built to Avoid Blame

Many institutions operate within cultures shaped by risk avoidance rather than learning.

Hospitals worry about recidivism metrics and reimbursement penalties. Community programs fear losing funding if outcomes appear poor. Law enforcement agencies fear scrutiny following use-of-force incidents. Providers struggle under overwhelming caseloads and inadequate staffing.

Under those pressures, systems often focus on protecting themselves first.

THIS CAN CREATE ENVIRONMENTS WHERE:

- difficult patients are avoided
- families are excluded
- communication weakens
- crises escalate unnecessarily
- transparency disappears

People living with severe mental illness frequently become trapped inside these fractures.

No single provider intends harm. The collective result can still be devastating.

Accountability Is Not the Same as Punishment

True accountability is not about assigning shame.

It is about creating systems capable of learning.

Every industry that manages complex risk depends on accountability structures:

- aviation

- public health
- engineering
- emergency response

When failures occur, those systems study what happened carefully in order to prevent future harm.

Mental health systems should function the same way.

Families deserve:

- transparent communication
- meaningful review processes
- opportunities to report systemic failures
- honest evaluation of adverse outcomes
- measurable improvement efforts

Without accountability, systems repeat the same mistakes while families continue paying the price.

The Human Cost of Silence

One of the most painful experiences for caregivers is feeling invisible after harm occurs.

Families often leave psychiatric crises carrying unanswered questions:

- Why was treatment denied?
- Why was someone discharged too early?
- Why did communication break down?
- Why did no one intervene sooner?
- Why was jail used instead of treatment?

Silence deepens trauma.

People can survive difficult truths more easily than institutional avoidance. Honest conversations create opportunities for healing and improvement. Defensive systems create resentment and distrust.

Communities cannot repair what they refuse to examine.

Building Trauma-Informed Accountability

Accountability structures themselves should be trauma-informed.

Families reporting concerns are often doing so after years of crisis, fear, and emotional exhaustion. Individuals living with mental illness may already distrust institutions due to previous experiences of coercion or mistreatment.

Trauma-informed accountability means:

- listening carefully
- responding respectfully
- reducing defensiveness
- prioritizing problem-solving
- acknowledging harm honestly

This approach strengthens systems rather than weakening them.

Transparency builds trust.

Oversight and Continuous Improvement

Mental health systems need stronger mechanisms for evaluation and improvement.

Communities should consider:

- independent oversight offices
- ombudsman programs
- public reporting dashboards
- family feedback systems
- crisis outcome reviews
- cross-system coordination audits

Data matters, but lived experience matters too.

A program may appear successful statistically while families continue experiencing serious barriers to care. Both forms of information are essential.

Communities improve when they are willing to examine uncomfortable truths honestly and openly.

Supporting the Workforce While Improving Systems

Accountability must also recognize the realities facing frontline workers.

Many providers operate under impossible conditions:

- understaffing
- burnout
- inadequate reimbursement
- high trauma exposure
- overwhelming caseloads

Blaming individual workers for systemic failures rarely produces meaningful change.

Healthcare workers, case managers, peer specialists, police officers, judges, and emergency responders often function inside systems already stretched beyond capacity.

Reform must support the workforce while improving the structures surrounding them.

The goal is not punishment.

The goal is better outcomes.

Families like mine do not expect perfection from mental health systems.

We do hope for honesty, humility, and a willingness to learn when harm occurs.

Accountability is not about finding someone to blame for every tragedy. It is about building systems capable of responding differently next time.

Communities grow stronger when they stop protecting broken processes and start protecting people instead.

Real accountability asks a simple question:

"What can we learn from this so fewer families suffer the same outcome?"

25

A Blueprint for What's Next

After years of navigating mental health systems, one truth has become impossible for me to ignore: we already know enough to do better.

Communities across the country have piloted programs that reduce incarceration, stabilize housing, improve treatment engagement, and save lives. Researchers have spent decades studying what supports recovery. Families have been describing the same gaps for generations. Individuals living with serious mental illness have repeatedly told systems what helps and what harms.

The problem is no longer a lack of knowledge.

The problem is fragmentation, hesitation, and the absence of coordinated action.

Too often, reform efforts appear in isolated pieces. One county creates a mobile crisis team while another expands supportive housing. One hospital improves discharge planning while another launches peer support services. Small pockets of innovation emerge while the larger system remains disconnected.

Real transformation requires something broader.

It requires a blueprint.

Building a Full Continuum of Care

Mental health systems cannot function effectively when every service operates independently.

Crisis response, hospitalization, outpatient treatment, housing, peer support, transportation, family engagement, and long-term stabilization must work as connected parts of the same structure.

Families experience the consequences when those systems fail to communicate.

A person may stabilize briefly inside a hospital only to be discharged into homelessness. Someone may receive medication during incarceration but lose treatment access immediately after release. Families may finally secure an outpatient appointment months after the crisis that made the appointment necessary has already passed.

The system repeatedly reacts instead of coordinating.

A stronger continuum of care would allow individuals to move between levels of support without constantly falling through gaps. Crisis care would connect directly to outpatient stabilization. Housing systems would coordinate with treatment teams. Families would receive guidance rather than being left to navigate fragmented systems alone.

Many communities already know how to build these structures. What remains uncertain is whether we are willing to prioritize them.

Shifting From Crisis Management to Prevention

For decades, much of mental health policy has centered on reacting to collapse.

We wait for hospitalization.

We wait for incarceration.

We wait for psychosis to intensify.

We wait for homelessness.

We wait for tragedy.

Then we mobilize enormous resources in response.

A healthier system would invest far earlier.

Early identification in schools, coordinated outpatient treatment, family education, housing support, peer navigation, and community-based intervention consistently produce stronger long-term outcomes than repeated emergency response.

Prevention rarely attracts public attention. Successful prevention often looks invisible. The crisis never occurs. The arrest never happens. The hospitalization is avoided quietly before it begins.

That kind of success matters deeply even when headlines never acknowledge it.

Designing Systems Around Human Reality

Policies often fail when they are designed around ideal behavior rather than human reality.

People living with severe mental illness may struggle with insight, consistency, transportation, memory, organization, or trust. Families may be exhausted, financially strained, and emotionally overwhelmed. Providers may carry impossible caseloads inside systems burdened by workforce shortages.

Effective systems acknowledge those realities and are designed to respond to them.

Appointments must become easier to access. Crisis systems must become easier to navigate. Communication between agencies must improve. Services must continue long enough for trust and stability to develop.

A fragmented system expects vulnerable people to navigate complexity during moments of crisis.

A humane system reduces that complexity instead.

The Role of Communities

Federal legislation matters. State funding matters. National reform matters.

Local communities matter too.

Some of the most meaningful changes in behavioral health have begun at the county and city level. Judges have launched behavioral health dockets. Sheriffs have partnered with treatment providers. Hospitals have integrated peer support specialists. Counties have expanded diversion programs and crisis stabilization units.

Communities do not need to solve every problem at once in order to begin moving in the right direction.

Progress often begins with a few leaders willing to ask different questions.

What if jail was not the default response?

What if housing became part of healthcare planning?

What if families were treated as partners?

What if individuals with lived experience helped design the system itself?

Questions like these create openings for change.

Rebuilding Trust

One of the deepest wounds within mental health systems is the erosion of trust.

Families lose trust after repeated failed interventions. Individuals living with severe mental illness lose trust after traumatic hospitalizations, frightening police encounters, forced treatment experiences, or prolonged instability. Providers lose trust in systems that leave them overworked and unsupported.

Rebuilding trust requires more than policy reform.

It requires transparency. Consistency. Communication. Respect.

People are more willing to engage with systems that treat them with dignity rather than suspicion. Families are more willing to collaborate when they feel heard instead of dismissed. Providers function more effectively when systems support sustainable care rather than constant crisis management.

Trust grows slowly.

Systems must become worthy of it again.

The Future We Choose

Mental health reform is often framed as a political issue, a healthcare issue, or a budget issue.

At its core, it is a human issue.

Every policy decision eventually reaches someone sitting in an emergency room beside a loved one in psychosis. Every funding decision affects whether a family receives support or silence. Every legal standard shapes whether intervention happens early enough to prevent collapse.

Families like mine live inside the consequences of those decisions every day.

The future is not predetermined. Communities can continue

building systems centered around fragmentation, incarceration, and emergency response. Communities can also choose something different.

We can build systems organized around stability, treatment, dignity, prevention, and connection.

That future is possible.

The question is whether we are finally willing to build it.

For much of Jonathan's life, I kept searching for the one program, the one hospital, the one intervention that might finally change everything.

Over time, I realized the deeper problem was never one missing piece.

The problem was that the pieces rarely worked together.

Real reform requires more than isolated solutions. It requires systems capable of functioning as a connected whole. Families should not have to become case managers, investigators, advocates, and emergency coordinators simply to keep someone alive.

People living with serious mental illness deserve systems designed for recovery instead of survival.

Much of the blueprint already exists.

Now comes the harder part.

Choosing to build it.

Sources

Serious Mental Illness and Anosognosia

Amador, Xavier. *I Am Not Sick, I Don't Need Help! How to Help Someone with Mental Illness Accept Treatment*. Vida Press.

Treatment Advocacy Center. "Serious Mental Illness and Anosognosia."

Treatment Advocacy Center. "Research Weekly: Anosognosia and Treatment Refusal."

National Institute of Mental Health (NIMH). "Schizophrenia."

National Institute of Mental Health (NIMH). "Bipolar Disorder."

American Psychiatric Association. *Diagnostic and Statistical Manual of Mental Disorders (DSM-5-TR)*. American Psychiatric Publishing.

Criminalization of Mental Illness

Treatment Advocacy Center

Treatment Advocacy Center. *Serious Mental Illness and Jail Diversion.*

Council of State Governments Justice Center. *Improving Outcomes for People with Mental Illnesses Involved with New York City's Criminal Court and Correction Systems.*

Bureau of Justice Statistics. *Indicators of Mental Health Problems Reported by Prisoners and Jail Inmates.*

National Alliance on Mental Illness (NAMI). *Jailing People with Mental Illness.*

Substance Abuse and Mental Health Services Administration (SAMHSA). *Behavioral Health Barometer Reports.*

Homelessness and Serious Mental Illness

National Alliance to End Homelessness

National Alliance to End Homelessness. *State of Homelessness Reports.*

United States Interagency Council on Homelessness. *Ending Homelessness Among People with Serious Mental Illness.*

SAMHSA. *Permanent Supportive Housing Evidence-Based Practices Toolkit.*

Crisis Response and Mobile Crisis Teams

SAMHSA 988 Lifeline Resources

SAMHSA. *National Guidelines for Behavioral Health Crisis Care.*

White Bird Clinic. *CAHOOTS Program Reports.*

White Bird Clinic (CAHOOTS)

Denver STAR Program Reports.

National Council for Mental Wellbeing. *Roadmap to the Ideal Crisis System.*

Assisted Outpatient Treatment (AOT)

Treatment Advocacy Center. *Assisted Outpatient Treatment Research.*

New York State Office of Mental Health

New York State Office of Mental Health. *Kendra's Law Program Evaluations.*

California CARE Court Resources.

Kentucky Tim's Law Legislative Materials.

Mental Health Courts and Diversion Programs

Council of State Governments Justice Center. *Behavioral Health Diversion and Mental Health Courts.*

Miami-Dade Criminal Mental Health Project Reports.

Eleventh Judicial Circuit of Florida Mental Health Project

Stepping Up Initiative Publications.

Stepping Up Initiative

Housing and Recovery Models

SAMHSA. *Permanent Supportive Housing Toolkit.*

National Alliance to End Homelessness. *Housing First Evidence Summary.*

United States Department of Housing and Urban Development (HUD). *Housing First and Supportive Housing Resources.*

Corporation for Supportive Housing. *Supportive Housing Evidence Base.*

ACT (Assertive Community Treatment)

SAMHSA. *Assertive Community Treatment Evidence-Based Practices Toolkit.*

National Alliance on Mental Illness. *ACT Team Resources.*

Substance Abuse and Mental Health Services Administration. *Evidence-Based Resource Guide Series.*

Family Engagement and Caregiver Support

National Alliance on Mental Illness (NAMI). *Family-to-Family Program Materials.*

SAMHSA. *Engaging Families in Behavioral Health Care.*

Family Run Executive Director Leadership Association (FREDLA).

Mental Health Policy and Systems Reform

SAMHSA.

National Council for Mental Wellbeing.

Council of State Governments Justice Center.

The Kennedy Forum.

The Bazelon Center for Mental Health Law.

National Association of Counties (NACo).

American Psychiatric Association.

Federal Policy and Medicaid

Centers for Medicare & Medicaid Services (CMS).

United States Congress. Congressional Research Service Reports on:

- IMD Exclusion
- Medicaid Behavioral Health Services
- Community Mental Health Funding

Congress.gov

Legal Issues, HIPAA, and Civil Commitment

United States Department of Health and Human Services.

HHS HIPAA Guidance

Treatment Advocacy Center. *Civil Commitment Standards by State.*

Bazelon Center for Mental Health Law.

Kentucky Revised Statutes (Tim's Law).

California CARE Court Statutes.

New York Kendra's Law Statutes.

Recommended Reading

Xavier Amador. *I Am Not Sick, I Don't Need Help!*

Xavier Amador. *Becoming Fluent in LEAP - How to Get to Partnering.*

Pete Earley. *Crazy: A Father's Search Through America's Mental Health Madness.*

Torrey, E. Fuller. *American Psychosis.*

Torrey, E. Fuller. *Surviving Schizophrenia.*

Greiling, Mindy. *Fix What You Can: Schizophrenia and a Lawmaker's Fight For Her Son*

Jaffe, DJ. *insane consequences: How The Mental Health Industry Fails The Mentally Ill.*

Patrick J. Kennedy and Stephen Fried. *A Common Struggle.*

Rosenberg, Kenneth Paul, MD. Bedlam: An Intimate Journey Into America's Mental Health Crisis.

Elyn Saks. *The Center Cannot Hold.*

Nanos, Lynn, L.I.C.S.W. *Breakdown: A Clinician's Experience In A Broken System Of Emergency Psychiatry.*

Glossary

REFERENCED MENTAL HEALTH, LEGAL, AND SYSTEMS TERMS

ACT (Assertive Community Treatment)

A team-based mental health treatment model designed for individuals with severe mental illness who need intensive support. ACT teams often include psychiatrists, nurses, social workers, case managers, and peer specialists who provide services directly in the community.

AOT (Assisted Outpatient Treatment)

A court-ordered outpatient treatment program for individuals with severe mental illness who have a history of repeated hospitalizations, homelessness, or involvement with the criminal justice system. The goal is to help people remain stable and connected to treatment while living in the community.

Anosognosia

A neurological symptom associated with some serious mental illnesses that prevents a person from recognizing they are ill. It is not denial or stubbornness. The brain is unable to accurately perceive the illness itself.

Behavioral Health Docket

A specialized court program that works with individuals living with mental illness who have become involved in the justice system. The focus is on treatment, accountability, and recovery rather than punishment.

Behavioral Health Court

See Mental Health Court.

CARE Court

A California court-based program designed to connect individuals living with severe mental illness to treatment, housing, and supportive services through structured care plans.

Case Management

A service that helps individuals coordinate treatment, housing, benefits, transportation, employment supports, and other resources needed for recovery and stability.

Case Manager

A professional responsible for helping individuals access and coordinate services and supports.

Civil Commitment

A legal process allowing courts to order psychiatric treatment when an individual meets specific criteria established by state law.

CIT (Crisis Intervention Team)

A specialized training program that teaches law enforcement officers how to safely and effectively respond to people experiencing mental health crises.

Community-Based Treatment

Mental health services provided within a person's community rather than in a hospital or institutional setting.

Continuum of Care

A coordinated system of services that supports individuals through different levels of treatment, housing, recovery, and long-term support.

Court-Ordered Treatment

Mental health treatment required through a court process, often used when an individual is unable to recognize their need for care.

Criminalization of Mental Illness

The practice of responding to symptoms of mental illness through arrest, incarceration, court involvement, or law enforcement intervention rather than through treatment, healthcare, housing, and supportive services.

Crisis Stabilization Unit (CSU)

A short-term treatment facility designed to help individuals experiencing psychiatric crises stabilize in a safe, therapeutic environment without requiring hospitalization or incarceration.

Delusion

A fixed belief that remains unchanged despite clear evidence that it is not true. Delusions are a common symptom of psychotic disorders.

Diversion Program

A program that redirects individuals away from incarceration and toward treatment, housing, and supportive services.

Emergency Detention

A temporary legal process allowing a person experiencing a severe psychiatric crisis to be held for evaluation and treatment.

Florid Psychosis

A severe state of psychosis characterized by intense hallucinations, paranoia, delusions, and disorganized thinking.

Functional Decline

A significant decrease in a person's ability to manage daily life activities, work, relationships, self-care, or independent living due to illness.

Grave Disability

A legal standard used in some states describing a person who, because of mental illness, cannot provide for basic needs such as food, shelter, safety, clothing, or medical care.

Hallucination

A sensory experience that occurs without an external source. Hallucinations may involve hearing voices, seeing things, smelling odors, or experiencing sensations that are not actually present.

HIPAA

The Health Insurance Portability and Accountability Act. A federal law that protects medical privacy while allowing certain information sharing under specific circumstances.

Housing First

An evidence-based approach that prioritizes stable housing before requiring individuals to address mental health, substance use, employment, or other challenges.

IMD Exclusion

A federal Medicaid policy limiting reimbursement for treatment provided in larger psychiatric facilities serving adults between ages 21 and 64. Many advocates believe this policy contributes to shortages in psychiatric treatment beds.

Involuntary Commitment

A legal process allowing psychiatric treatment when an individual meets state-established criteria and cannot safely care for themselves.

Jail Diversion

Programs that redirect individuals with mental illness away from incarceration and into treatment and support services.

Kendra's Law

A New York law authorizing Assisted Outpatient Treatment for certain individuals with severe mental illness who meet specific legal criteria.

LEAP

A communication approach developed by Dr. Xavier Amador. LEAP stands for Listen, Empathize, Agree, and Partner. The model helps families and professionals build trust with individuals who do not recognize they are ill.

Medicaid

A government-funded healthcare program that provides medical and behavioral health coverage for eligible individuals and families.

Mental Health Court

A specialized court designed to connect eligible individuals living with mental illness to treatment and support rather than traditional incarceration.

Mobile Crisis Team

A team of mental health professionals who respond directly to psychiatric crises in the community to provide assessment, de-escalation, and connections to services.

Peer Respite

A voluntary, short-term crisis support program staffed by individuals with lived experience of mental illness and recovery.

Peer Support Specialist

An individual with lived experience of mental illness, recovery, or caregiving who is trained to support others facing similar challenges.

Permanent Supportive Housing

Long-term housing paired with ongoing support services such as case management, treatment support, and life-skills assistance.

Pretrial Diversion

A program allowing eligible individuals to receive treatment and supervision instead of proceeding through traditional criminal court processes.

Psychiatric Advance Directive

A legal document that allows individuals to state treatment preferences in advance of a future mental health crisis.

Psychiatric Boarding

The practice of holding individuals in emergency departments while waiting for psychiatric placement due to shortages of available treatment beds.

Psychiatric Emergency

A mental health crisis requiring immediate intervention to protect an individual's safety or well-being.

Psychiatric Hold

A temporary legal detention allowing mental health professionals to evaluate and stabilize a person experiencing a psychiatric crisis.

Psychiatric Urgent Care

A behavioral health clinic designed to provide immediate mental health assessment and treatment without requiring hospitalization.

Psychosis

A condition that affects a person's perception of reality and may include hallucinations, delusions, paranoia, and disorganized thinking.

Recovery

A personal process of managing mental illness, building stability, and pursuing a meaningful life. Recovery does not necessarily mean symptoms disappear completely.

Recidivism

The repeated return to a system after intervention. In criminal justice, it refers to repeated arrests or incarceration. In healthcare, it may refer to repeated hospitalizations.

Schizophrenia

A serious brain disorder that affects thinking, perception, emotions, behavior, and the ability to distinguish reality from psychosis.

Self-Neglect

The inability or unwillingness to meet basic personal needs such as food, shelter, medical care, hygiene, or safety due to mental or physical impairment.

Sequential Intercept Model

A framework identifying key points where individuals with mental illness can be diverted from the criminal justice system and connected to treatment.

Serious Mental Illness (SMI)

A mental health condition that substantially interferes with major life activities. Examples include schizophrenia, schizoaffective disorder, bipolar disorder, and severe major depression.

Stabilization

The process of reducing acute psychiatric symptoms and restoring a person's ability to function safely and effectively.

Supportive Housing

Affordable housing paired with supportive services that help individuals maintain stability and independence.

Tim's Law

A Kentucky law that authorizes court-ordered outpatient treatment for certain individuals living with severe mental illness who meet established criteria.

Trauma-Informed Care

An approach to care that recognizes the impact of trauma and seeks to avoid re-traumatization while promoting safety, trust, and healing.

Value-Based Care

A healthcare payment model that rewards providers for improved outcomes rather than simply the number of services delivered.

Wraparound Services

A coordinated set of supports that may include treatment, housing, transportation, employment assistance, peer support, family services, and other resources designed to meet an individual's comprehensive needs.

988 Suicide and Crisis Lifeline

The national three-digit crisis number connecting individuals experiencing mental health, substance use, or suicidal crises with trained crisis counselors.

About the Author

Kimberly A. Bowman is an advocate, speaker, and systems reformer dedicated to improving the lives of individuals and families affected by severe mental illness.

Her work is rooted in both lived and professional experience. As the mother of an adult son living with severe mental illness, Kimberly has spent decades navigating the realities of psychiatric crises, treatment gaps, homelessness, justice involvement, and the heartbreaking consequences of a fragmented system of care. Those experiences transformed her from caregiver to advocate and fueled a lifelong commitment to building better solutions for families facing similar challenges.

Professionally, Kimberly has served in leadership roles across behavioral health, psychiatric services, nonprofit management, public policy, and community advocacy. She has worked alongside law enforcement, mental health professionals, policymakers, and first responders to improve crisis response, expand access to care, and advance meaningful systems change. She is also actively involved in Crisis Intervention Training (CIT) initiatives and founded programs supporting first responder wellness through certified canine therapy.

Through her writing, speaking, and advocacy, Kimberly challenges the assumption that the failures surrounding severe mental illness are inevitable. She believes that individuals experiencing psychiatric illness deserve treatment instead of criminalization, support instead of abandonment, and systems designed around recovery rather than crisis.

The System We Never Built reflects both her family's journey and her vision for creating the compassionate, coordinated, and accountable system of care that individuals and families have deserved all along.

www.ingramcontent.com/pod-product-compliance
Lightning Source LLC
LaVergne TN
LVHW040519210926
848480LV00007BA/1513

9781961605725